The Bible Code:
A Journey to Judgment Day

Dan Harlap

Equidistant Publishing

Equidistant Publishing
P.O.Box 6255
Marion Bridge
Nova Scotia B1K 3T8
Canada
www.equidistant.ca

Cover illustrations:
Fragments from MS. Laud Or. 321 folio 91 verso, Germany, c. 1275.
Courtesy of The Bodleian Library, University of Oxford, UK.

Printed in Canada

Canadian Cataloguing in Publication Data

Harlap, Dan, 1947-
The Bible code : a journey to judgment day

Includes bibliographical references.
Includes matrices in Hebrew.
ISBN 0-9688035-0-4

1. Judgment Day—Biblical teaching. 2. Bible. O.T.
Pentateuch—Criticism, interpretation, etc., Jewish. I. Title.

BS1225.6.E75H37 2001   296.3'3   C00-901529-9

*In the hope that the light
seen by this book returns
to the Creator
and brings Him happiness*

Contents

Acknowledgements

I am grateful to professor Eliyahu Rips for his generous help and support. His comments have greatly contributed to my understanding of the Bible Code. Throughout my research and writing of this book, his positive attitude, honesty and sensitivity have been a source of illumination.

I am indebted to Dr. Alexander Rotenberg for developing and making available to me the state-of-the-art software to research the Code. Without this software I would never have been able to delve into the depths of the Code, nor publish my discoveries.

Many thanks to Dr. Leib Schwartzman for sharing with me a few of his discoveries.

I wish to thank professor Robert Haralick for offering his help and valuable comments.

I am thankful to Barry Roffman for sharing his experiences with me, for providing a few calculations, and for general advice.

I thank these five members of The International Torah Code Society, of which I am proud to be a member. Due to the sensitive nature of issues discussed in this paperback, I did not ask any of them to endorse this book prior to its publication. Only professor Robert Haralick and Barry Roffman read the manuscript, and not for endorsement purposes. At the time, in addition to registering the manuscript with The Canadian Intellectual Property Office, I asked professor Haralick and Mr. Roffman to safeguard two copies of the manuscript for copyright purposes.

I thank Mary-Adah Curbera, Patricia Conway and Paula Mickalik who read earlier versions of parts of the manuscript. Very special appreciation to Brenda Conroy for very helpful editorial assistance of the final manuscript.

My son Jonathan made it possible for me to mark matrices electronically, for which he deserves my deepest gratitude.

"I want to know God's thoughts…
the rest are details."

Albert Einstein

Chapter 1
The End of Days

I have always had a Bible in my office. I had meant to read the Torah once more, but time went by, and I did not get around to do it. I have always believed in God and cherished the spiritual man who lives in me. Yet, having grown up in a secular home, I was not an observant Jew. A few years ago, circumstances put me in touch with a friend who used to live in Madrid and later moved to Sydney, Australia. She had become a very religious person and a casual e-mail led to a lengthy conversation about religion, God, beliefs and life in general. Every few days lovely e-mails made their way between Spain and Australia via a server in California, and an old friendship was rekindled. She urged me to read the Bible, especially since I know Hebrew and, therefore, would be able to read the Old Testament in its original language. As I had had in mind to reread it, I decided to dedicate an hour a day to reading the Bible. In a few days I finished reading the Torah and enjoyed the experience immensely. It so happened that a few days later I switched on the TV just at a time when someone was speaking about the Bible Code. It sounded fascinating and, being a spiritually oriented person, these comments made a lot of sense to me. Something told me that a lot of information had been encoded in the Torah for me to decipher. Three weeks later I flew to Canada via Amsterdam, and as I walked into the airport's bookstore, my eyes spotted Michael Drosnin's book *The Bible Code*. By the time the airplane landed in Montreal, I knew my life had changed. In Europe again, I delved into the subject, and a mind-boggling experience began to unfold.

When I first read the book and saw two or three matrices, I immediately noticed that the Torah is a text which had been written in three dimensions. Years ago I had traded future markets and always wondered how to plot a price chart in three dimensions. Frequently, prices move without any fundamental reason, something which means that economists can only partially explain a price movement.

Obviously, a price represents the aggregate expectations of all market participants at a certain moment, and some of those expectations are impossible to measure. I devoted a long time to researching what I called "everything which causes a price to move but cannot be explained nor measured by an economist." I called the component economists cannot measure a third dimension. I chose to represent that dimension by a mathematical equation which took into account the daily price range in relation to planet Mercury's heliocentric daily speed. I looked for a mathematical coefficient, one which would have a relation to nature, to our solar system, and would be a variant, not a constant. Therefore, I chose planet Mercury, for it is the fastest planet in our solar system and has the most variable heliocentric speed. Basically, this coefficient is a sine wave which, calculated by a certain mathematical equation, determines the width of a day on a price chart. That is, instead of plotting a simple bar chart, my program plots a daily price chart whereby each day has a different width, which represents the third dimension. (The results of that research were published in a short article called "Short-term price progression explained by a third dimension" in *Cycles* magazine, volume 45, number 6, May 1996.) Hence, after meditating for years on how to produce a three-dimensional price chart of what we normally see as a two-dimensional price/time chart, I find it convenient to think of the Torah Code in three dimensions.

Creating a price chart in this manner demonstrates that variations in daily price ranges affect the velocity of time. By this I mean that an event can make the specific time which correlates to a specific commodity or stock go faster. Every matter and every person has its own pace, its own code of evolution and therefore, its own time. This behooves that there are many types of "time." Evidently, human beings on planet Earth relate to time as a derivative of our solar system. We refer to a year when planet Earth completes a whole circle around the sun. The Hebrew calendar calls a month when the moon circles once around Earth. This is one type of time by which we measure the sequential relation that one event has to another. This finding brought me to ask myself how God sees time. Obviously, for One who looks at us from outside the solar system, time is something else, especially when

He sees a few worlds. It seems that instead of time, God monitors a progress of events. Interestingly, the Torah Code confirms this concept. The minimal skip in the Torah of the term *future time*, זמן עתיד, -279, coincides with the textual phrase *all the past*. This suggests that what for us is future, for someone else is past. Or in other words, there is a different world which is ahead of us in time, a world which already went through the events we are experiencing today. In the same way, what for us is past, for someone else is future. This means that there is yet a different world behind us which is now experiencing events that we already went through. Consequently, there are a few worlds which, at the same "time," experience events which belong in different time windows. And this is how, for God, a sequence of events move forward. This matrix suggests that this has always been and always will be the case, for the phrase *throughout your generations* crosses the term *future time*. It is significant that one line below is encoded the word *event*, מאורע, in skip -10, and the text which is written in this line reads as follows: *A cubit shall be its length, and a cubit its breath, four square shall it be*. This phrase suggests that the different worlds are spaced out in equal number of events, not equal time, from each other. An numeric example is also provided in this matrix. Crossing *future time* is written *two hundred and fifty… two hundred and fifty… five hundred.*

○ *future time* ◌ *all the past* ⌐ *throughout your generations*
□ *event* ⌐⌐ *two hundred and fifty* ⬠ *five hundred*
___ *a cubit shall be its length, and a cubit its breath, four square shall it be*

Interestingly, in Hebrew, the gematria (numerology) of the word *past* is 272 and the gematria of the word *future* is 484. When we locate the number 484 above the number 272, in this form

484

272

we can see a symbolic visualization of the division of the worlds. The right side (2,4) represents the past, the existence of a world in distance 2 events behind us and another one trailing us in distance of 4 events. The left side (2,4) represents the future, the existence of a world 2 events ahead of us and another world which is 4 events ahead of us. The number 7 is our world and the number 8 is a parallel world above us. According to Kabbalah, above us exists an identical world to ours. This is the origin of the phrase "as above, so is below." The difference between 7 and 8 symbolizes that the identical world above is slightly ahead of us. It is slightly ahead of us because, by granting us free choice, God does not know if tomorrow a person will choose good or evil. Nonetheless, knowing all possible outcomes, God knows what will happen if a person chooses righteousness and He knows what will ensue if one chooses wickedness. As such, God needed an identical world to ours which will be one event ahead of us so He can better monitor what is happening on planet Earth. Thus, it seems that there are six worlds. Two are ahead of us, two are behind us, and one is parallel and slightly ahead of ours. The minimal appearance of the term *six worlds*, ששה עלמות, is encoded in the Torah in skip 1218. According to Kabbalah, God created and destroyed many worlds which existed before ours in an attempt to create a world which will contain the correct mixture of mercy and justice. Only a world which contains such perfect balance is able to be propelled forward by perpetual goodness. It is possible that our universe is the third generation of such a multidimensional attempt, for the phrase *three times* coincides with *six worlds* as well as the term *third generation*.

Training my mind to see price charts in three dimensions made it possible for me to visualize the Torah as a three-dimensional text. In this way I am able to understand the position of matrices in the structure. Later, while thinking about the Dead Sea Scrolls, it occurred to me that perhaps the Essenes concealed the scrolls

רובבלאשרתשאלכנפשכואכלתשמלפנייהוהואלהיכושמחתאתהוביתכוהלו
תעשהכנלאיקשהבעינכבשלחכאתוחפשמענמככימשנהשכרשכירעבדכשששנ
עשהידיכיהויתאכשמחשלושפעמימןמיהיראהכלזכורכאתפנייהוהאלהי
איזידונעודכיתבאאלהארצאשריהוהאלהיכנתנלכוירשתהוישבתהבהוא
האלהיכאליותשמעונכבכלאשרתמענמיהוהאלהיכבחרבבימהמהקהללאמר
דמהנהקימישראלוטובלבכלאשתידלכלאתסיגגבולרעכאשרגבלוראשנימבנחלתכאשרת
כמאדאשרלאמעריהגויימהאלההנהרקמעריהעמימהאלהאשריהוהאלהיכנת
מהנחילותאתבנילאתאשריהיהלולאישכללבכראתבנהאהובהלפנייבנהשנ
השערהואמראביהנערהאלהזקנימאתבתינתתילאישהזהלאשהויושנאהוהנה
יגרהייתבארצובנצונימאשרילדולדהמדורשלישידובאלהמבנקהליהוהיכיתצא
אשתואשרלקהלחלאיחבלרחיימורכבכינפשהואחבלכיימצאאישגנבנפשמאחי

○ six worlds   ⊔ three times   ⊓ third generation

in the shape of a cylinder on purpose, to convey a message, not only for the reason that in Qumran there was no lack of space in the caves where the scrolls were found. The Essenes could perfectly well have concealed the texts in rectangular boxes. Rather, they chose to hide them in jars, a difficult task taking into account that a few of the scrolls are made of copper. The earliest the Dead Sea Scrolls are dated by scholars is 250 BC and the latest 68 AD. This means that the Essenes concealed the scrolls about one thousand years after the Torah had been given to the Jewish people. It is possible the Essenes knew about the Torah's being encoded and wished to convey a secret message by shaping the texts as three-dimensional cylinders. The message is that, as the Torah was written in a continuous spiral of letters, a plethora of information is stored in multidirectional cross-sections. Thereafter, I realized that the Torah was actually written as a three-dimensional cone, not a cylinder. I pondered about the graphical curved shape of the stone tablets with which Moses is depicted descending from mountain Sinai. These tablets are shaped as if they were a section of a three-dimensional cone. The sides of the stone tablets were straight, in parallel, but the curved tops serve as an indication that the stones are a vertical cross-section cut out of a cone. In a cone, as the vertical cross-sections become lower, their circumference becomes larger. Researching the Code, the higher we go in skip sequences, the fewer the number of lines the Torah contains, and the longer they are. This observation supports my theory that God created the

Torah as a continuous spiral of 304,805 letters in the shape of a three-dimensional cone. It is significant that a complex text such as the five books of the Torah was originally written in Hebrew without vowels. In the Hebrew language, alternating vowels assign different meanings to a word. Furthermore, when text is written without vowels and without spaces, a phrase can have more than one meaning. An exquisite example can be found in Exodus 6:22. This verse contains three names, *Misha'el, and Elzafan and Sitri. And...,* ...ו וסתרי מישאל ואלצפן. God made sure that when this line is written without spaces, the line reads *and they will inquire into the code and its mysteries*, ישאלו אל צפן וסתריו.

A note on the existing translations of the Masoretic Hebrew text of the Torah into the English: At times, a verse was translated to the English phonetically rather than by interpreting the literal text. For example, Genesis 41:45 is written in Hebrew as צפנת פענח, which means *decipher the code*. The term *decipher the code* is extremely important, for God intended to convey a message about the Torah being encoded. This expression appears only once in the Torah. When Joseph was in Egypt and solved the dream of The Pharaoh, he was awarded the name *Joseph decipher the code*. In fact, it is surprising that Joseph was given this name, for he deciphered The Pharaoh's dream, not code. Evidently, there is a clear message in naming Joseph *Joseph decipher the code*. Alas, the translation to the English reads *Zaphenat pa'aneah*, as it sounds in Hebrew. Consequently, a person who does not speak Hebrew cannot understand what is written in this verse. In such cases I used the literal translation and wrote in brackets, 'my translation'. I also used my translation in cases where a phrase may be understood in more than one way, or when reading the Torah without spaces, a line may be read differently. A note on English grammar: At times, a Hebrew word is translated into two English words. In such cases I wrote "word," in singular, even though two or more English words followed.

The Torah is known to contain five books; Genesis, Exodus, Leviticus, Numbers and Deuteronomy. However, in reality, the Torah contains six books. The sixth book consists of all the information that is encoded in the five books. The fact that a sixth book exists in the Torah can be seen in the following matrix. The minimal appearance of the words *sixth book*, ספר שישי, in skip -2192, coincides with the phrase *inscribed with the finger of God*. Another meaningful phrase addresses the issue of sealing the sixth book, similarly to what is written in the book of Daniel, chapter 12, verse 4, where Daniel is given the following instruction: *But you, Daniel, shut up the words, and seal the book, until the time of the end: many shall run to and fro, and knowledge shall increase*. In the same chapter, in verses 8 and 9 the same theme is repeated: *I heard, but I did not understand. Then I said, O my Lord, what shall be the issue of these things? He said, Go your way, Daniel, for the words are shut up and sealed until the time of the end*. In this matrix, the verse that crosses the words *sixth book* speaks about locks: *…and he made the middle lock in order to lock inside…* (my translation). One line below is encoded the word *end* in skip 2, just before the word *encoded*, and the word *destruction* in skip 3 is encoded in the same line. The word *destruction* is encoded here in its minimal skip in the Torah. This line seems to say that in the sixth book the end is encoded, and it is about destruction. Interestingly, the word *God's book* is also encoded in this matrix, sharing the first letter of the words *sixth book*. The words *God's book* are encoded back to back in its minimal skip in the Torah, 2188.

○ sixth book   △ God's book   □ end   ⌐ encoded
⬛ inscribed with the finger of God   ◇ destruction
___ and he made the middle lock in order to lock inside

In his book, *Y. Leibowitz: Ideas and Contradictions* (1994), Moshe Gilboa quotes professor Yeshayahu Leibowitz: "The entire Torah is in our hands and nothing of it is left in heaven. We are not permitted to wait for a new revelation of the holy spirit to solve our problems. In the Torah, which was given to us, there must be found a solution for everything and it is up to us to extract it from the text." I doubt that professor Leibowitz had the Code in mind when he wrote these lines but in my opinion, he defined precisely the function of the Torah Code. With this in mind I approached the Code, understanding that the Code enables me to decipher a setting which God had encoded in the Torah.

The existence of the Code was already known hundreds of years ago. Rabbi Moshe Cordevaro (1522-1570, known as *Ramak*) wrote in *Pardes Rimonim*: "The secrets of our holy Torah are revealed through knowledge of combinations, gematria (numerology), switching letters, first-and-last letters, shapes of letters, first and last verses, *skipping of letters* (*dilug otiot, in Hebrew*) and letter combinations. These matters are powerful, hidden and enormous secrets. Because of their great hiddenness, we do not have the ability to fully comprehend them" (italics are mine). The *Gaon* (genius) from Vilna (1720-1797) writes in his commentary on *Sifra d'Tzniusa* (Concealed Book): "The rule is that all that was is and will be, until the end of time, is included in the Torah from [the first word of the Torah] '*Bereishis*' to [the last words of the Torah] '*l'eynei kol Yisrael*'. And not merely in a general sense, but including the details of every species and every person individually, and the most minute details of his life from the day of his birth until his death." The Kabbalist Aryeh Kaplan writes in his book *Meditation and Kabbalah* about manipulation or permutation (*tzeruf otiot*) of letters. He mentions that Rabbi Judah Albotini (1453-1519), in his book *Sulam HaAliya* (Ladder of Ascent) referred to skipping of letters: "Another idea that Albotini discussed in detail is that of 'jumping' (*kefitza*) and 'skipping' (*dilug*). Although this is mentioned by Abulafia [Rabbi Abraham Abulafia, 1240-?], and the method was absolutely used by him, he does not present a clear picture how one makes use of it." The great teacher of the *Ramban*, Rabbi Eliezer (Rokeach), in the introduction to his commentary on the Torah, describes "73 ways to understand and interpret the letters of the Torah." Number 54 is called "the way of skipping." As well, an example of encoding by equidistant letter sequences is explicitly mentioned in a commentary on the Torah written by Rabbi Bachya in 1291 (chapter 1, verse 2). Kabbalists taught us that God created the universe with the Hebrew alphabet. According to Jewish mysticism, "The Torah has always been viewed by Jews as a map of all existence through space and time, standing outside and above it. The physical world is the Torah's derivative, not the other way around. And it is, in particular, the *letters* of the Torah that, in some mysterious way, are God's agency for the world's creation." (Satinover, 1997).

During the last few years, Code researchers have found numerous historical events encoded in the Torah. In 1988, the physicist Doron Witztum published an important book called *Hameimad Hanosaf* (*The Additional Dimension*), in which numerous matrices deal with phenomena of the Torah itself, of Jewish holidays, of the French Revolution, of Jewish sages, of the Dryfuss trial, of the Holocaust and of diseases like diabetes and AIDS. In 1989, Rabbi Shmuel Yaniv wrote a book called *Secrets in the Torah*. Later, a significant article was published in *Statistical Science* (1994) by Eliyahu Rips, Doron Witztum and Yoav Rosenberg. It is titled "Equidistant Letter Sequences in the Book of Genesis" and deals with the appearance of names of Jewish sages in close proximity to their dates of birth or death. Professor Daniel Michelson, a mathematician from The Weizmann Institute published an excellent article "Reading the Torah with Equal Intervals." In 1996, a book by Dr. Moshe Katz, *On Hidden Codes in the Torah*, was published in Israel. Many matrices describe the Holocaust, the Gulf War and current affairs. In 1997 Dr. Jeffrey Satinover wrote an interesting book, *Cracking the Bible Code*, which analyzes the Bible Code specifically and codes in general. Another book which saw the light in 1997 is *Actuality in Skipping Letters in the Torah*, by professor Robert Haralick and Rabbi Matityahu Gerlson. This book deals with two systems of encoding; the Torah Code and gematria.

In our modern era, during the first half of this century, Rabbi Chaim Michael Dov Weissmandl extensively researched the Code by writing the Torah on 10x10 cards. Counting letters is easier when the Torah is written on cards containing 100 letters each. Nonetheless, only with the advent of computers has the meticulous research of the Code become feasible. Apparently, God chose to reveal Himself via the Torah, whether via the plain text or via the Code, both of equal importance.

One wonders why the Torah contains words which are misspelled or distorted. In the Bible published by Koren Editions, these words are written without vowels. To the best of my understanding, a word in the Torah is often spelled in a way to facilitate the Code. For example, in Genesis 27:22, we read that Jacob went to his old father Isaac to steal his blessing from his older brother Esau while the latter was out hunting. Isaac was already blind and had to touch Jacob with his hands in order to identify who it was he was blessing. While touching his son, Isaac said: *The voice is Jacob's voice, but the hands are the hands of Esau*. The first word *voice* is written in two letters, missing the Hebrew letter *vav* (חסר חולם), and the second *voice* in three letters, with the letter *vav* (חולם מלא). Why is it written this way? Obviously God could not use a letter *vav* in the first one for it did not harmonize with the Code. There are many words in the Torah which at times are spelled with or without the letters *vav* or *yod*, always to facilitate the Code. Moreover, at times, a word is spelled with an additional letter or a different one for that purpose. For example, in Genesis 27:3, the word *hunting* is written with an additional letter ה because God needed a fourth letter there to facilitate the Code. He chose an ה, either because the letter ה was specifically needed there, or because the letter ה distorts the word *hunting* in the minimal way. Similar distortions of other words appear in Genesis 14:2, Genesis 24:33, Genesis 25:23, Genesis 30:11 and in many more instances. God surely knew that *Rashi* (Rabbi Shlomo Yitzhaki) and other Jewish sages would comprehend those meanings in the plain text, but clearly He recognized the supreme importance of the Code and chose to sustain its accuracy. Likewise, God knew there would be many skeptics of the validity of the Code and therefore, if a distortion were necessary, He opted for the Code's accuracy rather than the accuracy of the plain text. Professor Eliyahu Rips is quoted in Drosnin's book, saying that God wrote the Torah in a flash. Not only do I think that God did not write it in a flash, but I think that it was difficult for Him to create such a multidimensional text. The fact that God had to misspell words in the plain text to facilitate the Code serves as proof that the task was difficult.

For the ones who are unfamiliar with the Torah Code, the mechanics of the Code are as follows: The five books of the Torah are combined into one continuous string of 304,805 letters without spaces between them. We then search for a word in a range of equidistant skip sequences. If the word is encoded in equal intervals, the program writes the Torah continuously, each line containing a number of letters equal to the skip sequence. In other words, the Code turns the Torah into a dynamic text, albeit without disturbing the order of letters in which the text was written. For example, the term *spiritual world*, עולם רוחני, written as one word, is encoded in its minimal skip sequence in the Torah of 170. The program rewrites the Torah on one large page containing 1793 lines of 170 letters each, except from the last line which contains only 1788 letters (that is, 1793x170+1788=304,805 letters). Therefore, somewhere on this page the word *spiritual world* עולם רוחני, is written vertically. One would then look for relevant information which comprises the word *spiritual world* and the text surrounding it, whether in plain text or in code. Consequently, reading a matrix is a two-dimensional interpretation. The general rule is that a minimal skip sequence or near-minimal skips of an encoded word or phrase are more important than non-minimal skips. Nonetheless, this is not always the case. A name of a person, for example, may be encoded a few times, relating to different aspects of the person's life. Another rule has to do with the proximity of relevant information to an encoded word or phrase. Professor Robert Haralick from the Department of Electrical Engineering at the University of Washington suggests the following rules: In order for a pair of ELSs (Equidistant Letter Sequences) to show up in the same matrix, one of three things has to occur: (1) They both have small skips and appear horizontally; in this case they must be near to each other in lineal text distance. (2) One must have a small skip so that it appears horizontally and the other appears vertically or near vertically; in this case the cylinder size must be related to the skip intervals of the larger skip ELS; the relationships that work are s, s+1, s-1, s+2, s-2, s/2 s/2+1, s/2-1, s/2-2, s/2+2 and so on, and where the smaller skip ELS is lineally harmonically close to one of the letters of the larger skip ELS. (3) Both ELSs are larger skip ELSs; in this case, their skip intervals must be harmonically related (as in music) so that there is some cylinder size that will work for both of them and some letter of one ELS must be in a lineal harmonic closeness to some letter of the other ELS.

This method is only the beginning of the equidistant system, for one has to go a step further and not ignore the rest of the text outside the matrix. To decode a setting, a scenario, one needs numerous matrices which are linked and interweave because a single, isolated matrix will not suffice. Accordingly, in my mind, I entwine the rest of the text and create numerous matrices in front and behind the specific matrix I found. In this way, I see the text as a cube containing matrices suspended in air and as I walk around, above, below and within the cube, there are many possible planes where related information can be found and reproduced on a two-dimensional matrix. In a two-dimensional world, a Torah Code matrix generated by a specific word is defined by its skip sequence. In a three-dimensional world, a matrix generated by a specific word is defined by the angle from which one looks at the cube.

Our covenant with God, the Absolute Good, stipulates: *Love your neighbour as yourself* (Leviticus 19:18). Unfortunately, in our society we encounter egoism, greed, indifference and cruelty. Moral values and social justice have almost ceased to exist. People treat money as sacred instead of as secular, and as a result, the main forces that drive society are greed and wickedness. Furthermore, the vast majority of Jewish people do not abide by the covenant. Knowing human nature, God understood that human beings were unlikely to love their neighbours as they loved themselves. Thus, He warned us in the Torah of the dire consequences of not abiding by the covenant. God created a beautiful world so that human beings may experience full and wonderful lives, provided human behaviour is guided by perpetual goodness. This, however, behooves that if the world advances by perpetual wickedness, God does not have an obligation to maintain it. In the Torah, God wrote explicitly that although He is a merciful God, He is also a revengeful one.

God wanted to see a world in which perpetual goodness is the motor that moves the world forward. He wanted people to help each other, show solidarity and be charitable. God tried to achieve this goal by saving a people from slavery. After agreeing, a priori, to live according to His laws, God imposed on His chosen people a religion called Judaism. Jewish people were to comply with 613 precepts. (The six hundred thirteen precepts are divided into 248 positive commandments and 365 negative ones. This division parallels the 248 limbs and 365 sinews in the human body.) The covenant bonds the two, God and Jewish people, for eternity, and it contains harsh warnings: *And if by this discipline you are not turned to me, but walk contrary to me, then I also will walk contrary to you, and I myself will smite you sevenfold for your sins* (Leviticus 26:23,24).

Rabbi Mordechai Kamenetzky explains that "The Torah, in painting the scene at Sinai, places the Jews in a very strange location in relation to Mt. Sinai. *And the Jews stood under the mountain* (Exodus 19:17). The wording is strange. The Torah should have written that the Jews stood at the foot of the mountain or at the bottom of the mountain. The wording *under the mountain* seems to be unsuitable.

The Talmud in Tractate Shabbos explains this verse in a literal sense. Hashem, the Talmud explains, literally placed the Jews under the mountain by lifting the mountain above them like a giant pot! And in that state, the Talmud continues, Hashem decreed, 'If you will accept the Torah, fine. However, if you do not accept the Torah, this will become your final resting place.' …The Torah, the Maharal of Prague (1526-1609) explains, is a vital necessity for worldly existence. It is more than the blueprint of creation, it is the raison dêtre of the entire universe. And its presentation had to personify such. Though there was unmitigated love and wholehearted enthusiasm in the Jewish nation's acceptance of the Torah, Hashem had to make a point that would be as eternally powerful as Torah itself. He presented the Torah with unmitigated force – a manner that characterized its essence – a vital necessity for mortal and universal existence. Torah's acceptance could not be left to the fortunate goodwill of a very spiritual and wanting nation. It was wonderful that the Jews accepted the Torah as such, and their acceptance merited endless reward. But it was time to show what the Torah truly meant to the creation at large. Otherwise, for generations, the emergence and observance of Torah would be an outcome of mortal benevolence – and that is not the case." (Kamenetzky, 1997).

Amid thunder, lightning, loud sound, fire and smoke which engulfed Mount Sinai, God gave the Torah to His chosen people. Judaism was born, the religion which was designed to illuminate the souls and direct the lives of all Jewish people and subsequently of all human beings. As a result of saving the people from slavery and proclaiming them chosen people, God, the sublime Benefactor, has a moral claim on the gratitude and obedience of His chosen people. Judaism was the first religion that required people to love God, to love Him with all our hearts, with all our souls and with all our might. God commanded us to love Him not for His egoistical needs. Rather, God understood that when a person loves God, that person acquires high moral values and therefore, becomes a better human being. Unfortunately, only a fraction of the Jewish people live according to the Torah, and the secular State of Israel, the nation of Jewish people, has been the exact opposite of what God intended it to be. As such, it looks like the "chosen people" experiment has failed. As a result, the Torah Code suggests that the Lights have now decided to implement Judgment Day. Not surprisingly, the Code reveals that we are rapidly approaching the time slot where calamity is scheduled.

There are two matrices which demonstrate that God not only warned the Jewish people in the plain text of the Torah that He would avenge them for breaking the covenant, but that He also encoded His intention to avenge them. In the following matrix you can see that the expression *the Lord avenged*, יהוה נקם, in its second-minimal skip, 336, coincides with the same theme written in plain text: *I will take vengeance*, אשיב נקם. Why would the Lord take vengeance? The answer is found in Deuteronomy 31:16: *…and they will forsake me and break my covenant.* God repeats this verse in 31:20 when He tells Moses that *they will turn to other Gods and serve them, and despise me and break my covenant.* The phrase *break my covenant* is written only twice in the Torah. These two instances coincide in this matrix with *the Lord avenged,* as well as the phrase *this Torah book.* God speaks to Moses about the people of Israel and indeed, *the people of Israel* also crosses the expression *the Lord avenged.* One line below the latter is written *the Rock of his salvation will wither. They stirred him to jealousy with strange gods; with abominable practises they provoked him to anger.*

האלהארצאאשרנשבעיהוהלאבתמלתתלהמואתהתנחילנהאותמויה
למעני למדוויראואתיהוהאלהיכמושמרולעשותאתכלדבריהתו
אשמהבקרבוועזבני והפראתבריתיאשרכרתיאתו וחרהאפיבובי
לאלהימאחרי מועבדומונאצוני והפראתבריתי והיהכיתמצאנא
תיהוהלאמרלקהאתספרהתורהזהתשמתמאתומצדארונברעיתיהו
אז ניכלקהלישראלאתדבריהשירהתהאתעדתממהאזינ והשמימוא
דובניאדמיצבגבלתעמימלמספרבני ישראלכי חלקיהוהעמוייעק
יטשאל והעשהורי נבלצורישעתוי קנאהובזרי מבתועבתיכעיסה
רעבולחמירשפוקטבמרירי ושנבהמתאשלחבמעמחמתזחלי עפרמח
ועננברירושאשכלתמרתתלמוחמתמתני נמיי נמוראשפתני מאכזרהל
אמשנותיברקחרבי ותאחזבמשפטי דאשי בנקמלצרי ולמשנאיאש
חיי כמוובדברהזהתהתארי כוריימימעלהאדמהאשראתמעברי מאתהירד
בני ישראלוזאתהברכהאשרברכמשהאי שהאלהי מאתבני ישראללפ

○ the Lord avenged
☐ I will take vengeance
__ break my covenant
- - - this Torah book
⌐ ⌐ the people of Israel
⌊__⌋ the Rock of his salvation will wither

Most people find it difficult to believe in the Torah Code. Evidently, they do not take God and His warnings seriously, as in modern society the Bible seems to be considered archaic and outdated. To most of us, God is something elusive people think about when they hope or seek help. Maybe the last matrix and the following one will bring a person to reconsider his beliefs, for they provide strong evidence that first, the Torah is intentionally encoded, and second, that no human being could have authored the Torah.

The Book of Leviticus, chapter 26, outlines numerous explicit warnings in case the Jewish people do not obey the rules of the covenant. In verse 25 God warns *And I will bring a sword upon you, that shall execute vengeance for the covenant.* The phrase *vengeance for the covenant* is written only once in the Torah in plain text. It is most impressive that God encoded the minimal skip in the Torah, 99, of the words *vengeance for the covenant*, נקם ברית, to coincide with the phrase *shall execute vengeance for the covenant*, נקמת נקם ברית. In this matrix the word *Israel* is encoded in skip -10. In the same line where the word *Israel* is encoded, is written *Then if you walk contrary to me, and will not hearken to me, I will bring more plagues upon you, sevenfold as many as your sins.* The other lines that cross the encoded words *vengeance for the covenant* spell the terrible outcome: *And make you few in number, so that your ways shall become desolate.... You shall eat the flesh of your sons, and you shall eat the flesh of your daughters.... And your cities shall be a waste.... And I will draw out after you the sword.*

רעכמואכלהואיביכמונתתיפניבכמונגפתמלפניאיביכמורדובכמשנ
האתכמשבעעלחטאתיכמושברתיאתגאונעזכמונתתיאתשמיכמכברזלוא
לאיתנפריוואמתלכועמיקריולאתאבולשמעליויספתיעליכממכהשבע
מתכמוהמעיטהאתכמונשמודרכיכמואמבאלהלאתוסרוליוהלכתמעמיק
מוהבאתיעליכמחרבנקמתנקמבריתונאספתמאלעריכמושלחתידברבתו
נוראחדוהשיבולחמכמבמשקלואכלתמולאתשבעוואמבזאתלאתשמעולי
עלחטאתיכמואכלתמבשרבניכמובשרבנתיכמתאכלווהשמדתיאתבמתי
נפשיאתכמונתתיאתעריכמחרבהוהשמותיאתמקדשיכמולאאריחבריחנ
מאזרהבגוימווהריקתיאחריכמחרבוהיתהארצכמשממהועריכמיהיוחר
בתהארצוהרצתאתשבתתיהכלימיהשמהתשבתאתאשרלאשבתהבשבתתיכמב
דפאתמקולעלהנדפונסומנסתחרבונפלוואינרדפוכשלואישבאחיוכמ
ימואכלהאתכמארצאיביכמוהנשארימבכמימקובעונמבארצתאיביכמו

○ *vengeance for the covenant*

▭ *shall execute vengeance for the covenant*

□ *Israel*

__ *then if you walk contrary to me, and will not hearken to me, I will bring more plagues upon you, sevenfold as many as your sins*

⌐¬ *you shall eat the flesh of your sons, and you shall eat the flesh of your daughters*

⬠ *and make you few in numbers*

└┘ *and your cities shall be a waste*

\- - - *and I will draw out after you the sword*

A few years ago, excellent Torah Code researchers in Israel found powerful evidence in the Code suggesting the destruction of the State of Israel in the year 1996. Apparently, the Code reveals such a possible outcome, but whether because Benjamin Netanyahu was Prime Minister at the time or another reason, a holocaust did not take place in 1996. This book suggests that the possible next holocaust is scheduled to take place in the very near future. An alarming and meaningful matrix shows the words *Judgment Day*, יום הדין, in its third-minimal appearance in the Torah, in skip -627, coinciding with the minimal appearance of the word *Lights*, מאורות, in skip 2, and with the term *nuclear holocaust*, שואה אטומית, in its only appearance in the Torah, in skip -3133. It is my understanding that a Council of a few entities called Lights govern the universe under the supervision of God, the Source of the Light. These few Lights are located in a circle below the Source of the Light and together create a cone shape of Luminaries. In this matrix, the encoded word *judgment* coincides with the word *judgment* in the text. In the same line is written *the Lord's vengeance*, a phrase which is written only once in the Torah. The phrase *and the Lord's anger burned against Israel* also coincides with *Judgment Day*. Crossing the words *Judgment Day* is written *the people of Israel* and *the army will die* (my translation). Just above the term *Judgment Day* is encoded in skip -1 the Hebrew word *I will destroy*. The importance of this matrix lies with the fact that the words *Judgment Day* coincide with the only appearance of the term *nuclear holocaust* and the minimal appearance of the word *Lights*. Furthermore, this matrix is significant because of the presence of a second system of encoding, namely gematria. The gematria of the words *Judgment Day* is 125 and the gematria of the word *Lights* is 653. Adding the two numbers we get 778, which is the gematria of the term *nuclear holocaust*. Professor Eliyahu Rips, a well known mathematician from the Hebrew University in Jerusalem, brought to my attention that what precedes the word *Lights* in skip 2 is indeed an abbreviatory form of the term *court of law*.

○ *judgment day*	△ *nuclear holocaust*	□ *Lights*
◇ *abbreviation of 'court of law'*	▭ *the Lord's vengeance*	⬠ *judgment*
⬠ *I will destroy*	⊏ *the army will die*	
___ *the people of Israel*	⊔ *and the Lord's anger burned against Israel*	

קראהדאילאחדכבשימבנישנהשבעהתמימימיהיולכמומנזהתמסל
שנימכבשימבנישנהארבעהעשרתמימיממומנחתמונסכילהמלפרים
יהלכמכלמלאכתעבדהלאתעשווהקרבתמעלהאשריחניחזחליהו
החרישלהוקמונדריהואסרהאשראסרהעלנפשהעלנפשיקמואמריומש
מדינלתתקמתיהוהבמחנהאלפלמטהאלפלמטהלכלמטותישראל
מכלנקבההנהנההיולבניישראלדברבלעעמלמסרמעלביהוהעל
אחדנפשמחממשהמאותמנהאדמונהבקרומנהחמרימונאהצאנממ
אלאשרחצהמחמשהמנהאנשימהצבאימותרימאתיהימצחתהעדהמנהאצאנשלש
לבניראובנולבניגדעצומאדדיראארדיראתאתהיראתארצהגלעל
הוהויחראפיהוהבישראלוירנעמנבמדברארבעימשנהעדתמכלהד
יצאמפיכמתעשוויואמרכמרגדובניראובנואלמשהלאמרעבדיכי
ימברצרוגדרתהצאננבניראובנבנונאתחשבונואתאלעלאואתקרי
וכהימהמדברהרויעלכודרכשלשתימימבמדברבראתמחריחנובמרהוי
ויסעומחרחהגדגדויחנויביטבתהויסעומיטבתהויחנובעברנה
מאתהירירדנאלארצכנענוהורשתמאתמשבכלישביהארצמפניכמואבד
בולימוהיהלכמהימהגדולוגבולוזהיהיהלכמגבולצפונזהימוזהיהי
הבנישמעונושמואלבנעמיהודלמטהבנימיזנאלידדבנכסלונולמ
נסמהההרצחועליהמתנוארבעימושתימעירכלהעריאשרתתנ
פגעורבוהואימתנוראמבשנאהכיהדפנואוהשליכעליויבצדיהורי
רמקלטולשלובשבתבארצעדמותהכהנהולאתחנפואתהארצאשרא
המתהיינהלכנשימולאתסבנחלהלבניישראלממטהאלמטהכיאיש
יושבעבעשתרתבאדעירבעברהירדנאברתירדנוהואילמשהבארת
אלאמרשמעבינאחכמוושפטתמצדקביניאישובינאחיובינגרו
תמראתאתפיהוהאלהיכרכומותרגנובאהאליכמותאמראומבשנאתיהוה
רנהעמדלפניכרהואיכהבאשמהאתהרחזקיהואיזקיהואלנהאתהישראלוט
שוהיושבימבשעירויראואמכמונשמרתממאדלאתתגרובמכילאא
המלחמההמקרבההמחנהכאשרנשבעיהוהלהמוגמידיהוההיתהבמל
מראעברהבראצכבדברכבדברכאלכלכלאסרימימיושמאולאכלבבספ
אעוגמלכהבשנלקראתנוהואוכלעמולמלחמהאדראיויאמריהו
תאישואתהארצהאזתאתירשנובעתההואמערערעלשערעלנחלארננוח
אתכלאשרעשהיהוהאלהיכמלכישנימהמלכיםאהאלהכניעשהיהוהלכ
אשרענכימצוואתהכמעניכמהראותאתאתאשרעשהיהוהבבעלפעור
הרבעראשאשרעדלבהשמימחשכעננוערפלויודבריהואליכמממתוכ
ארצהטוביהואשריהואלהיכנתנלכנחלהלכנחלהכיאנכימתבארצהזאתא
שחיתכולאישכחאתברירתאתבתיכאשרנשבעלהמכישראלנאלימימר
ולמענתאריכימעמעלהאדמהאשריהוהאלהיכנתנלככללהימימא
תאבתינורכרתיהואתהברירתהזאתאתיכיאנחנואלהפההיורמכ
צאכיהוהאלהיככמשמביזדחזקהובזרענטויהעלכנצוצכיהוהאלה
בראלינואתאכלאשרידבריהוהאלהינואליכנושמענועשינורוי
ריהוהאלהיאבתיכלכלכארצזבתחלבודבשכדברישראלעשימישראלאלהינ
תירוחקיואשרצוכעשימתהישרוהטובבעינייהוהלמענייטבל
יתולאתחננמולאתאתחתנבמבתכלאתתנלבנוובתולאתקחלבנכבי
אהבכוברככוהרבכוברכפריבטנכופריאדמתכדגנכותירשכוי
להיכלפניכמממההומגהלהעדהשמדמומנתנמלכיהמבידכוהא
רצטוהארצנחליממימעינתותהמתיצאימבבקעהובהרארצחטהו
כתאחריאלהימאחרימועבדתמדתמוהשתחוריתלהמהעדתימבכמהיורמכ

In his book *The Bible Code*, Michael Drosnin articulates about the term *nuclear holocaust* in skip -3133. In my opinion, it would be naïve to expect a relevant date to appear in close proximity to the expression *nuclear holocaust*. Not only is the Code subtle and delicate, but I believe that God intentionally encoded the Torah in a way that would require a lot more than an isolated matrix to understand a setting. Coinciding with *nuclear holocaust* you can see the encoded phrase *Heavens, your dead are dust*, שמים, מתיך עפר, in its minimal skip in the Torah. An additional encoded phrase in its minimal skip which coincides with the encoded word *Heavens* reads *come out, Heavens.* צאי לי, שמים. The word *Heavens* is encoded once more in close proximity. The text which coincides with the first line reads *so take good heed; do not contend with them*. In this context, *with them* means with Heavens, with God. In other words, this matrix conveys the following message: Do not contend with the One in heaven because He will set off a nuclear holocaust to destroy you. *So will the Lord do to all the kingdoms into which you are going over.*

```
אתבנייישראלבקנאתילכנאמרהנניינתנלואתהבריתישלומוהיתהלוולדזרעואחריוברירתכהנתעולמת
ואבעלירדניירחוובאלהלאהיהאישמפקודידמשהואהרנהכהנאשרפקדואתבניישראלבמדברסיניכיא
חדכבשימבניישנהשבעתהבעתהתמימימיהיולכמומנחתממסלתבלולהבשמנשלשהעשרנימלפרשניעשרנימלאיל
הנהנהיולבניישראלדברלבדלעמלמסרמעלבהוהעלדרבפעורותהיהמנפהגעדתיהוהועתהתהרהרנוכל
יכמתעשוריאמרבניגדובנייראובנייראונבנאלמשהולאמיעבדיכיעשואשראדנימצוהפנישינומקנןנווכל
ימוהיהלכמהיהמהגדולדולדיהזיהיהזהויהיהתהלכמגמלבהדימיהוזהויהלהלכמגבולצפונומניהימהגדולדתתאולכמהר
מתהייינהלישימולאתהסבנוחלהלכבנייישראלממטהלאלמטהכיאישבנחלתמטהאבותיוידבקובנייישראלרכ
עשוהייישבמבשעירמהרהויראומסכומנשמרתמהאלמאתאלתהתנגרובמכילאאתנלכבמארצמעדמהאאתנלכבמארצמעדרכדפגלכירש
ראתאתכלאשרעשהיהוהאלהיכמלשנימלכיהאמריוהאשרהייהוהארצהמלכלהכלהמכיהמלכותאאשראתההעברשמהולאתי
אחריכולולמענתאריכימיכמעלהאדמהאשריהוהאלהיכנתנלכלכביהלכהימיהמיימאזיבדילמשהשלשערימבעברהי
היכמועודתיוזחקיואשרציווכיועשיתהישרוהטובבעינייהוהלכממעניייטבלכובאתוירשתאאתהארצהטבה
האלהיכוהלכתאתכלאלהיאמאחרימאחרימעובדתמותשחתמאתהולתלמהמהעדתיובמהוימכיאבדתאבדונכגרימאשר
שהמשפטויתומואלמנהואהבאהגרלתתלולחמושמלהואהבתמאתהגרכיגרימהיייתמבארצמצרימאתיהוהואה
שהכלאשראנכיימצוכורקבכלאותנופשכתנובחואכלתבשרכבכליחיכיכבתיהיההואלהיכאשרנתנלכלכלשעריכהוהמסמא
יכתתנננהואצללההואומכרלנכרייעמקדיושאתהליהיוהאלהילהיכלכיאתקימלכמלצמבהאשרנאיהיהוהאלהיכלאתזבחיהיהוהואלהי
הכלעצצלמיגזבחיהכירהאלהיאואלהיאושרתעשהעשהלכלכאשרתעשהעשהאשרנאיהיההואלהיכלאתזבחבחיהיהוהואלהי
ודשלשערימעימלהשלשהולשאלהלואלאישפכדמנקיבקרבצואכשרואשרבהיההואהאלהיכנתנלכלכלנתנלככלכלהיהלהויהיעליכדמימו
מהשבתתישיבמולמאחזיכואמדלמדלאקרובאחירכאליכולוליאישדעתוואספתואלתביתכוהיהעמכעדדרשאחיכואתו
```

○ *nuclear holocaust*

▢ *Heavens, your dead are dust*

△ *come out, Heavens*   ◇ *Heavens*

▭ *so take heed; do not contend with them*

__ *so will the Lord do to all the kingdoms into which are you going over*

Due to the dismal state of affairs on planet Earth, it is possible that the Lights have now decided that the holocaust scheduled during the year 5760 in the Hebrew calendar (2000) or shortly thereafter will indeed happen. The following matrix is generated by the minimal appearance of the words *holocaust brings destruction*, שואה הבא הרס, in skip -776. If letters are spaced differently, this phrase can also be read as *next holocaust*, שואה הבאה. Coinciding with *holocaust brings destruction* or *next holocaust* are written and encoded the year *760 (2000)*. The year in the Hebrew calendar can be shown as either 760 or 5760. The three letters of the year 760 are written in skip 1 only twice in the Torah. As well, the year 760 is encoded here again in skip -3. Crossing the words *holocaust brings destruction* or *next holocaust* is encoded the date *fifth of Nisan* and the word *subsequent to* coincides with it. This date is significant, for it is encoded here in its minimal skip in the Torah. The *fifth of Nisan* corresponds to April 10, 2000. According to this matrix, there was a possibility that the holocaust would have occurred in between April 10 and September 29, 2000. There is also a possibility that the date *fifth of Nisan* set off a chain of events which will lead to Judgment Day. The next few matrices will elaborate on the importance of the date *fifth of Nisan* and the events which followed suit.

○ *holocaust brings destruction, or,*

next holocaust

□ *fifth of Nisan*

__ *subsequent to*

△ ▭ *760 (2000)*

```
זבחההואתהחהזותואתשוקההימינהניפאהרנתנופהלפ
כמולהבדדילביהנהקדשובינהחלרובינהטמאורבינהטה
המהאשרעלהארצכלמפרסתפהטסרהשסותעופרסתממעל
ממעללרגליורלנתרבהנעלהאריצצאתאלהמהמתאכלואת
לכלזרעזרועעאשרירזרעטהורההראוכירותנמימעלזרע
יטהרהרובמלאתימיטהרהלבנאולבתתביאכבשבנשנת
ורוהיאהפכהשערלבבלבנומחיתבשרחיבשאתצרעתנושנ
נבברהתשערלבבנושפלהאינהמנהעורוהואכההוהס
רהואראישכייימרטראשוקרחתהאטהורהוראואממפאת
משניתורראהההכהנאאחריהכבסאתהנכנגעוהנהלאהפכהנ
אתכלשערואתראשוראתזקנונראתנגבתעייורואתכלש
חדאשמלתנרופהלכפרעליורועשורונסלתאחדבלולבשמ
נואתהביתבטרמיבאהכהנלראותאתאתהנגעולאיטמאכ
הארזואתהאזבואתשנהשניהתולעתואתהצפרהחייוטבל
```

The Code attributes significance to the month of Nisan, 760 (2000). I have been aware of the encoding of the coming holocaust for some time, but during the month of Nisan there had been a possibility that a certain event would serve as a sign. The sign would have been a guarding signal or at least an indication that the holocaust would be delayed. The following matrix shows the only place in the Torah where the word *in Nisan*, בניסן is encoded twice in close proximity. The year *760* coincides with the date, as well as the minimal skip, 62, of the phrase *a sign will protect*. The word *save* in plain text crosses the encoded word *protect*.

○ ◌ *in Nisan*
⬠ *760 (2000)*
☐ *a sign will protect*
___ *save*

The previous matrix which is generated by the phrase *holocaust brings destruction*, or *next holocaust* in skip -776, contains the minimal skip of the encoded date *fifth of Nisan*, April 10, and the word *subsequent to*, אחרי, coincides with this date. The matrix suggests that the holocaust is scheduled for after the fifth of Nisan, but there is also one more piece of information in this line. In Hebrew, the word

אחרי, subsequent to, contains the word ירח, which means month, or moon (in the Hebrew calendar, a month represents one moon's journey around Earth). In other words, this line points to another date, 'one month following the fifth of Nisan', which is the fifth of Iyar, May 10.

In the following matrix, you can see that the encoding of the Gregorian date, May 10, עשר במאי, coincides with the Hebrew one, fifth of Iyar. The minimal skip of the phrase *tenth of May*, 59, coincides with *fifth of Iyar* and the year *5760* (2000). The Hebrew word *fixed time* is written in close proximity, as well as is the encoded word *holocaust*. The name of the country *Syria* is encoded in close proximity in skip 3.

ושירועשיעגוותואלהבקררצאאברהמוריקהבנבבקררכוט
תאתוריקהחמאהוחלבובנגהבקראשרעשהוריתנלפניה
אכלווריאמרואליואיהשרויהאשתכוריאמרהנהבאהלוי
הנהבנלשרהאשתכוושרהשמעתפתחהאהלוהואאחרייוו
ימחדללהיותלשרהארחכנשימותצחקשרהבקרבהלאם
דניזקנוריאמריהוהאלאברהמלמהזהצחקהשרהלאמר
פלאמיהוהדברלמודעלבאאשוארילבכעתחיהולשרהבנו
ראהוריאמרלאכיצחקתדריקמומשמהאנשימוישקפועל
חמוריהוהאמרהמכסתאניזמאברהמאשראניעשהואברה
וונברכובובכלגוריהארצמדעתיולמענאשריצוהא
ודרכיהוהלעשותוצדקהומשפטלמענטיאריהועלאב
הוהזעקתסדמועמרהכירבההוחטאתמכיכבדהמאדארד
יעשורכלהראמלאאדעהויפנוומשמהאנשימוילכוסדם
והוירגשאברהמוריאמרהאפתסספהצדיקעמרשעאוליריש
תספהולאתשואלמקןומלמענחמשימהצדיקמאשרבקרבה
תצדיקעמרשעוריהיהכצדיקהכרשעחלללההשפטכלהאר

○ *tenth of May*
△ *fifth of Iyar*
▽ *5760 (2000)*
▭ *fixed time*
◇ *holocaust*
□ *Syria*

The manifestation of God seeing different worlds spaced in equal number of events, translates, every now and then, to significant dates spaced equally in time on planet Earth. The matrix which speaks about *future time* (page 11) contains the phrase *A cubit shall be its length, and a cubit its breath, four square shall it be,* and the word *event* is encoded in it. In other words, what we understand as "time" on planet Earth is "event" in cosmic perspective. As such, a chain of events being equally spaced in time on our planet is a derivative of different worlds being spaced in equal number of events.

A few matrices indicated to me that the event which was supposed to take place during the month of Nisan or on the fifth of Iyar could be the death of a president, possibly, the former president of Israel, Ezer Weitzman. President Weitzman was involved in a financial scandal, and during March and April 2000, the police investigation of monies he received from a French businessman intensified. The fifth of Iyar was Independence Day in Israel, and on that day president Ezer Weitzman collapsed during a ceremony. This event echoed the scenario I was alluding to, and a few days thereafter president Weitzman announced that he would resign on July 10, 2000, three years ahead of schedule. The State Attorney said that Weitzman's behaviour had raised serious ethical questions, and in the wake of political pressure that ensued he resigned. In March, I predicted that president Weitzman would die. Fortunately, I was mistaken. President Weitzman did not die, but his presidency did die. In addition, an important astronomical phenomenon took place in the heavens, when on May 10, 2000, a rare alignment of five planets was formed at 20 degrees Taurus. Ezer Weitzman relinquishing the presidency and the planetary alignment were not the end of that chain of events. The minimal skip of the date *fifth of Nisan* contains a time measurement of one month. Thirty days elapsed between the fifth of Nisan and the fifth of Iyar. As such, I expected a second event to happen thirty days following the fifth of Iyar. Astonishingly, precisely thirty days thereafter, on the sixth of Sivan, June 9, the president of Syria, Hafez Assad, died. The Torah Code brought me to believe that a president would die and that this event would have to do with the coming holocaust. As we know, one presidency died and one president did indeed die. Consequently, it looks like Assad's death postponed the holocaust.

The fact that the death of a president is associated with the holocaust can be seen in the following matrix. The minimal appearance of the phrase *a president will die*, נשיא ימות, in skip 735, coincides with the phrase *the holocaust is really coming*, השואה ממש באה, in skip -13. (Due to the length of this phrase, only part of it is visible in this matrix.) The word *will die* in text crosses *will die* in code. The year *5760* is encoded in close proximity.

צבעלעלתכואלכהאולייקרהיהוהלקראתיודברמהיראניוהגדתילכויל
מרקומבלקושמעהאזינהעדיבנוצפרלאאישאלויכזבובנאדמויתנחמהה
אשרמחזהשדייחזהנפלוגלועין{ו}ממהטבואהליכיעקבמשכנתיכישראל
ראלעשהחילוירדמיעקבוהאבי{ש}יןדמעירויראאתעמלקיישאמשלוויא
פינחסבנאלעזרבנאהרנהכהנהש{י}באתחמתימעלבניישראלבקנאואתקנא
תושלשימובניפלואליאבונב{אלי}יאבנמואלודתנואבירמהואדתנואב
מארבעהושמימאלפושלשמאותב{ו}ז{ו}בולנלמשפחתמ{סר}דמשפחתהסרדילא
אלפושמאותואלה{ב}ני{ד}נלמשפחתמ{שו}חממשפחת{שח}{מ}יאלהמשפחתדנל{מ}
תלויאשרילדהאתהלליולבמצר{ימח}{ד}לעמרמ{אה}רנואתמשהואתמרימא
תנחלהבתולכאחאביהמוהעברתא{תנ}חלתאב{יהו}להנואלבנייישראלתדברל
כלבנייישראלאתווכלהעדוהויעשמשהכאשרצוהיהוהאתוויקהאתיהושעו
יחנייחזאשהליהוהוהונסכיהמחציהיההנייהיהלפרושליישתההיןלאילורבי

○ *a president will die*
▭ *will die*
△ *5760 (2000)*
□ *the holocaust is really coming*

Assad's death is encoded in the following matrix. The minimal skip of the phrase *Assad's death*, מות אסד, -395, coincides with the minimal skip, 6, of the date *sixth of Sivan*, June 9. The year *5760* is encoded in close proximity, as well as the word *Syrian*.

ממצרימממבנעשריממשנהומעלהאתהאדמהאשרנשבעתילאברהמליצחקוליעקבכילאמלאואחרילבת
לאנשובאלבתינועדהתנחלבניישראלאישנחלתוכילאנחלאתמממעברליירדנוהלאהכיבאהנחלתנ
נימצוהטספניגנשיומקנינוכלבהמתנוריהיושמבערנוהגלעדועב{ד}כיעברוכלחלוצצבאבלפני{י}וי
להממשהלבנגדולבניראובנולחציעבטמנשבנויוספאתממלכתסיהנחנמלכהאמריואתממלכעתוגנמ
נחותיאירורונבהחהלכוירלכדאתקנתואתבנתיהויקראלהנחבשמט{ואל}המסעיבנייישראלאשר{י}צאומא
יהחירתועברועברותעברותהמדברהויוליכדרכשלשתימימבמד{בר}את{מ}וריחנוובמרהוי{עב}וומרהוויבא
בנ{נ}הויחנ{ו}ברסה{וי}סעומ{ס}ה{וי}חנ{ו}ב{וי}קהלתה{וי}סעומקהלתה{וי}סנ{וי}הרשפרויסעומהרשפרויחנוב
הרעלפייהוהיומתששמתבשנתהארבעימלצאתבניישראלמארצמצרימ{ב}חדשהחמישיבאחדלחדשואהרנ
להשטימעברבתמואביורידבריהואלהאלמשהובעברבתמואבעליירדנירחולאמרדבראלבנייישראלואמרתא
מעלהארצאשראתמעברימשביימבהוהיהיכאשרדמיתילעשותלהמאעשהלכמוידבריהוהאלמשהלאמרצואתב

○ *Assad's death*
□ *six of Sivan (June 9)*
◇ *5760 (2000)*
⬠ *Syrian*

An additional matrix which is generated by the expression *Assad is dead*, אסד מת, in skip -32, the second-minimal in the Torah, coincides with *Syria* and *a Syrian king*. The word *Syria* appears only once in skip 1 in the Torah. The date and year of Assad's death are encoded in close proximity.

חוצהויהיכשמעאדני ואתדברי אשתואשרדברה
אלי ולאמרכדברי מהאלהעשהלי עבדכ ויחראפו
וי קחאדני ו סמאתו וי תנהו ואלבי תהסהרמקו מ
אשראסורי הפלכאסורי מו י הי שבבי תהסהרוי
הי י הו האתי ו ספו י טאלי וחסד ויתנחנ ובעינ י
שרבי תהסהרוי תנשרבי תה סהרבי די ו ספאתכלה
אס רמא שבב י תה סהרו א תככלאשרעשי משמה ראה
י העשהאי נשרבי תהסהרראהאתכלמאומהבי דדוב
אשרי ה ו האתי ואשרהו אעשהי הומהצלי ח ו יהי א
חרהדברי מהאלהחטאומשקהמלכמצרי מו האפהל
אדני המלמלכמצרי מוי קצפפרעהעלשני סריסי
ועלשרהמשקי מועלשרהאופי מוי תנ אתמבמשמר
בי תרהטבחי מאלבי תהסהרמקואמאשרי הסמפאסו
רשמוי פקדשרהטבחי מאתי ו ספאתמוי שרתאתמו
יהיו רימי מבמשמרוי חלמוחלמשני המאי שחלמ

- ◯ *Assad is dead*
- ▭ *Syria*
- ⌐▭ ◇ *a Syrian king*
- ▢ *six of Sivan (June 9)*
- △ *760 (2000)*

The fifth of Nisan was the key date which set the sequence of events in motion. Accordingly, a third event was to take place a month following Assad's death. Indeed, July 10 was an eventful day. President Ezer Weitzman submitted his resignation, the Shas party quitted the coalition, leaving Ehud Barak with a minority government, and later in the evening, Prime Minister Barak left for Camp David where peace negotiations with the Palestinians were to reach a dead end.

These three dates, *fifth of Nisan* (April 10), *fifth of Iyar* (May 10), and *sixth of Sivan* (June 9), are encoded in close proximity in the following matrix. The year *760* coincides with the phrase *in that year*. The word *the crisis* is written here in plain text, suggesting the scenario which will unfold following this sequence of dates. The word *the crisis* is written only once in the Torah in skip 1. Concerning the fifth of Nisan, its importance may either emanate from a certain cosmic order that changed a month later as a result of the planets' alignment, or it is also possible that, secretly, a crucial decision was taken on that day by a head of state, the impact of which will become apparent in the future.

מלפיהטפולחמאינבכלהארצכיכבדהרעבמאדותלהארץ
מצרימוארצכנענמפניהרעבוריהעבוריהלקקטירוספאתכלהכספהנ
מצאבארצמצרימובארצכנענבשברהמשברוימויבאי
וספאתהכספביתהפרעהויתמהכםפמארצמצרימומארצכ
נענויבאוכלמצרימאליוילפלאמרהבהלנולחמולמהונמ
ותנגדככיאפססכספויאמריוסספהבומקניכמואתנהלכם
במקניכמאמאפסכספויבאואתמקניהמאליוספויתנל
המיוספלחמבסוסימובמקנההצאנובמקנההבקרובחמר
ימוינהלמבלחמבכלמקנהםבמבאשהההואותתמהשנההואואתה
ויבאואליובשנההשנינתויאמרולדלאנכחדמאדניכיא
מתמהכםפומקנההבהמהאלהמאלאדנילאנשארלפנייאדנילבלת
יאמגויתנוואדמתנוולמהנמותלעינינכגמאנחנוגמאד
מתנוקנהאתנווואתאדמתנוברלחמונהיהאנחנוואדמתנו

○ *fifth of Nisan (April 10)*

□ *fifth of Iyar (May 10)*

⬠ *sixth of Sivan (June 9)*

◇ *760 (2000)*

⊔ *the crisis*

▭ *in that year*

The postponement of the holocaust may have to do with the following matrix, which is generated by the minimal appearance of the expression *the sign of fifth of Nisan*, אות ה ניסן, in skip 11552. The line which crosses this expression depicts a time limit for redemption: *...if it is not redeemed within a full year*. Possibly, the holocaust was scheduled for the fifth of *Iyar*, 5760 (May 10, 2000), but a grace period of one year was awarded as a last chance for the people of Israel to conform with God's intentions as stipulated in the Torah. The grace period ends on the fifth of Nisan, 5761, or March 29, 2001.

טמאאהובנבלתבהמהטמאהאובנבלתשרצטמאורנעלמממנוורהואטמא
טהרהממקרדמיהזאתתורתהילדתלזכראולנקבהואמלאתתמצאידהד
תאביכללאתגלהשתבאביכהואערותאחיותאמכלאתתאגלהכישאראמכהו
ימימתהיהגאלתודואמלאינגאלעדמלאתלושנהתמימהדקמהביתאשר
פדוייהלויימאאתהבכורבבניישראליילקחתאתהכספפחמשהוששימוושלשמ
ומההואריאמרוהאנשימההמהאלירואנחנורטמאימלנפשאדמלמהנג
אהקדושרבלכמבנוילוייראמרמשהאלקרחשמעונאבניילוריהמעטמכ
יניכאשובהלידורואמרמלאכיהוהאלבלעמכעמהאנשימואפססאתהד
לאיקומריהויהוסאלחלכיהניאאביהאתהואמהיותהיהלאישונדר
וננעדהנהרהגדלונהרפרתראהנתתילפניכמאתהארצבאוורשואתהא
הואלהיכתירארואתואתעבדיובשמותשבעלעלאתלכונאחריאלהימאחר
נלכלשבתשמלאמריצאואנשימבניויבליעלמקרבכוידיחואתישביע

○ the sign of fifth of Nisan

▭ if it is not redeemed within one year

The following matrix supports my theory that the holocaust was scheduled for the fifth of Iyar but that God was merciful and awarded a grace period before Judgment Day comes into effect. The minimal appearance of the phrase *will have mercy for the sign of fifth Iyar*, ירחם אות ה אייר, is encoded in skip 5073 in the Book of Genesis. The line which crosses this phrase reveals God's reason for awarding the grace period: *Remember the everlasting covenant*. One line below and also crossing the expression *will have mercy for the sign of fifth Iyar* is written the word *war*.

ראאלהימכיטובויהיערבויהיבק
תמהללאלארבעימשנהושמנהמאות
ראיתיהלזכרברתעולמביגאלהי
לכגויימעשומלחמהאתהאתברעמלכסדמ
נותכחששרהלאמרלאצחקתיכייירא
אשימנוויפקאלהימאתעיניהות
לקחתאשהלבניויאמראלאדניאליל
עמימכאשראהבתיוהביאהליואכל
ותלדבנותאמתהפעמאודהאתיהוה
ורייפגעובומלאכיאלהימויאמרי
אלהימביתאלוסעומביתאלויהי
לולאשהיוראתהודהויחשבהלדז
וחמשאתארצמצימבשבעשניהשבע
שימולולבדוולהמלבדמולמצרים

○ will have mercy for the sign of fifth Iyar

▭ remember the everlasting covenant

— war

The following matrix combines the minimal appearance in the Torah of the term *Judgment Day*, יום הדין, in skip -39, with the phrase *the judgment of the Lights before the Lord*. Crossing *Judgment Day* is written *in its time, the people of Israel,* and the year *5760* is encoded here in skip 6. According to this matrix, sometime during the year 2000, a trial before God took place during which the Lights decided to implement Judgment Day.

```
כעלירולמענישמעניכלעדתבנייישראלולפנייאלעדזרהכ
הניעמדושאללהבמשפטהאוריהלפנייהוהיעלפיוייצא
ורועלפיריבאוהואוכלבנוישראלאתורכלהעדהוייעש
משהכאשרצוהיהוהאתויהקחאתיהושעויעמדהולפני
אלעזרהכהנולפניכלהעדהויסמכאתידיועליורייצו
הוכאשרדברירהוהבידמשהורידברייהוהאלמשהלאמרצו
אתבנייישראלואמרתאלהמאתקרבנילחמילאשירחני
חחיתשמרולהקריבליבמעדוואמרתלהמזההאשהאשר
תקריבוליהוהוהכבשימבנשנהתמיממשנימליומעלהת
מידאתהכבשאחדתעשהבבקרואתהכבשהשניתעשהביזה
ערבימועשיריתהאיפהסלתלמנחהבלולהבשמנכתיתר
ביעתההיינעלתתמידהעשיהבהרסינירלריחניחחאשהל
יהוהונסכורביעתההיינלכבשהאחדדבקדשהסכנסכשכר
ליהוהואתהכבשהשניתעשהביינתערבימכמנחתהובקרו
```

○ *judgment day*

▭ *the judgment of the Lights before the Lord*

⌐┘ *in its time*

‾ *the people of Israel*

☐ *5760 (2000)*

The words *there will be destruction*, יהי חתת, are written in the Torah once in plain text. In this matrix, these words are encoded in skip -43, and one line above is written the word *fixed time*. The year *5760* (2000) or the year 5766 (October 2005 to September 2006) is encoded in its minimal skip -11, coinciding with *there will be destruction*.

ריאראלויידבריהוהאלמשהלאמרצואתבניישראלויקחואל
יכשמנזיתזככתיתלמאורלהעלתנרתמידמחוצלפרכתהעדת
באהלמועדיערכאתואהרנמערבעדבקרלפנייהוהתמידחקת
עולמלדתתיכמעלהמנרההטהרהיערכאתהנרותלפנייהוהת
מידולקחתסלתואפיתאתהשתימעשרהחלותשניעשרנימיהי
ההחלההאחתושמתאותמשתימממערכותהשהמערכתעלהשלחנה
טהרלפנייוהונתהעלהמערכתלבנהזכהוהיהללחמלאזכ
רהאשהליהוהביומהשבתביומהשבתיערכנולפנייהוהתמי
דמאתבנישראלברייתעולםלמוהיתהלאהרנולבניוואכלהוב
מקומקדשכיקדשקדשימהואלומאשייהוהחקעולמויצאבנא
שהישראליתוהואבננאישמצריבתוכבבניישראלוינצובמחנ

○ *there will be destruction*

▭ *fixed time*

▢ *5760/5766 (2000/2006)*

God granted Man free choice while hoping that the engine which would set progress in motion would be perpetual goodness. This is why it is written in the Book of Genesis that God created Man in his image. Being the Absolute Good, God was hoping that His goodness would pass to Man, and therefore, Man would be built in God's image. We can read in the Book of Exodus 33:19 that when Moses asks God to show him His image, God answers *I will cause all my goodness to pass before your face*. God knew that in order for human beings to function by perpetual goodness, He would have to provide them a guide for life. For a long time He had looked for a people who would accept, a priori, to live according to His laws, according to His book. Alas, it appears that none of those primitive ancient societies were willing to undertake such an obligation to a God who was too abstract for them to believe in. Being a merciful God and seeing the suffering of a people who had been in slavery in Egypt for more than four hundred years, He decided to save them by performing great miracles in the hope that the people would recognize His existence and as a result, would be willing to undertake to live according to His laws. What ensued is described in the Book of Exodus. Finally, He had found a people who would be willing to abide by His covenant. He walked them in the desert for three months, and at Mount Sinai Moses informed Him that the people undertook, together, to do all that God would order them to do.

At that point, 3,313 years ago, God had to write a guide for life. He was aware of the fact that the guide, the Torah, would have a universal and eternal value. Therefore, before writing the Torah, He scanned His blueprint in order to identify sensitive branches He might have to address. We need to understand two cornerstones in God's philosophy: First, God established laws of nature which set our universe in motion. He then created Man who conducts himself in accordance to human nature. The outcome of this combination, laws of nature acting simultaneously with human nature, is what determines the course of life on planet Earth. In Hebrew we say this as "the world behaves as it does," עולם כמנהגו נוהג. As laws of nature represent the clock by which our universe ticks, and as human nature is fairly predictable, using Kabbalistic terminology of roots and branches we can say that there is an inherent logic in the way branches grow. In other words, God created a blueprint of creation, and at any time He can scan the blueprint and see what possible futures entail from each situation. God gave us free choice which means, by definition, that He does not know if tomorrow a person will decide to be righteous or wicked. In other words, at any point in time there is more than one possible future. Free choice is one of Judaism's cornerstones and indeed, the story of Adam and Eve in Garden of Eden is about free choice par excellence. God granted us free choice, but knowing all possible outcomes, God knows what will happen if a person chooses to be righteous and He knows what will ensue if he chooses to be wicked. The Talmud says that *everything is foreseen but the choice is given.* If everything is foreseen, how can we have a choice? And if we do have a choice, how can something be foreseen? One way to sort out this dichotomy is by saying that life is like a corridor and as one walks down the hall, one encounters doors. Behind each door dwells a setting, a scenario for you. Settings are entirely foreseen; which door to open is your choice. Every setting contains sub-settings, and somehow, life makes sure a person gets to these doors. Entering a door is a qualitative action whereby the distance a person walks in his setting is quantitative, for it measures the extent to which he realizes his potential. By choosing good or evil, as Ramchal explains, we are pulling from above a form of energy which had been set forth. The world of souls reacts to a person's choice by making available to him a path which God foresaw at the time of creation.

Second, since giving the Torah to the Jewish people at Mount Sinai, God's philosophy has been to diminish His intervention in our lives as time goes by. God's interference and time were always to be in inverse relationship. Apparently, God did not intend to baby-sit us for eternity. At the beginning, following the Exodus, the Jewish people were poor and they lacked infrastructure. God knew that He would have to be available to Moses for quite a while, but thereafter, during the periods of Judges, Kings, and Prophets, He would gradually reduce His direct involvement with our lives. He decided that the prophet Daniel would be the last one who would see an angel with his own eyes, and thereafter, if and when His interference was needed, He would interfere without people knowing about it. Already hundreds of years ago Jewish sages understood that God does not intervene readily in the affairs of this world. He gave us free choice, and He undertook to preserve our freedom. Only in extreme cases, whatever God defines as extreme, will He interfere in our affairs. It has been repeatedly emphasized that just because there are fools who spoil things on this planet, God has not been willing to change the order of our world. We now live in a period when people's choices are not only unevenly spread across the blueprint, but a great deal of them have crystallized, converged into a narrow area, in tandem with extremely powerful natural forces. From our point of view, such times result in upheaval and violent conflicts that bring major changes to society. From God's point of view, such times are more predictable.

In Biblical times, when the people of Israel did what was evil in the sight of the Lord, He gave them into the hands of their enemies. Measures to correct their behaviour, in case the Jewish people did not abide by the covenant, were incorporated into the blueprint. In order for His chosen people to serve as an example to the nations, אור לגויים, they first needed to live according to the Torah. We can safely assume that tragic events like the Babylon captivity, the exile of Jews to Babylonia in 597-538 BC, were supposed to serve as reminders to Jews to abide by the covenant. The lesson of the terrible persecution of Jews in the second half of the 14th century, after a third of Europeans died in the Black Plague, was that a Jew must help a Jew. The Spanish Inquisition and the expulsion of the Jews in 1492 was perhaps one more warning. The pogroms in Russia constituted a further reminder that we, Jewish people, need to abide by the contract, for *The Lord our God made a covenant with us* (Deuteronomy 5:2). It is difficult to make such harsh statements, but it seems that the terrible Holocaust which took place about half a century ago was, once more, a reminder that Jewish people must live according to *Love your neighbour as yourself*. Most likely, God was hoping that after such a horrific trauma, Jewish people who were finally to receive a country of their own, would live as God intended them to live, especially in the Holy Land.

Alas, in Israel, not only does a Jew not help a Jew, but hatred between orthodox and secular Jews has reached unprecedented levels. The gap between Ashkenazi and Sephardic Jews is wider than ever, and one million Russian immigrants are totally alienated. About sixteen percent of the population live below the poverty line. Poor manners and rudeness of Israelis foster a "dog eats dog" atmosphere. Needless to say, Israel today is the antithesis of what God intended it to be. It comes as no surprise that in His blueprint, God implemented a Judgment Day at the beginning of the Age of Aquarius.

The excellent Code researcher, Dr. Leib Schwartzman, brought to my attention that Ehud Barak's victory in the elections in 1999 is encoded in the Torah. The minimal appearance of the words *Barak will govern*, ימלוך ברק, in skip -63, coincided with the year *5759*, encoded in skip -11. Crossing *Barak will govern* is encoded in skip -2 the words *know the truth*. I noticed that in this matrix the words *know the truth* are encoded once more in skip -2. This time they cross the word *failure* which is encoded under the written word *peace*. This matrix suggests not only that Ehud Barak would be elected, but that the peace process will fail.

ישעלחמרוויישבווהעירהוייבאיהיודהואחיובביתהיוביתהיוספוהואעודנ
צהויאמרלהמיוספמההמעשההזהאשרעשיתמהלוואידעתמכינחשינ
מריהוודהמהנאמרלאדניימהנדברומהנצטדקקהאלהיממצאאתעונעב
ניגמאנחנוגמאשרנמצאהנמצאהגביעעבידודויאמרלהלימעשהותזאתה
בידזהוהואיהיהליעבדואתמעלולשלומאבלאברכמויגשאליוייהודה
נאעבדכדברברבאזניאדניואליחראפבבעבדזכביכמוככפרעהאדניש
שלכמאבאואחונאמראלאדניישלנוואבזקנווילדזקנימקטנוואחיו
אמרוואביואהבוותאמראאעבדכהורדהואלרקכהורדהואלרויואשימהעינינעליוו
להנערלעזבאתאבירוועזבאתאביוורמתותאמדאלעבדיכאמלאירדא
ספונלראותפנינייריהיכיעליונואלעבדכאברוונגדלואתדבריאדני
רולנומעטמאכלונאמרלאנוכללרדתאמישאחינוהוהקטנאתנוירדנ
ניהאישואחיונהקטנאיננונאתניוויאמרעבדכאביאלינוואתמידע
שתיוויצאהאחדמאתיוואמראכטרפטרפולאראיתיועדהנהולקחתמג

○ *Barak will govern*
□ *5759 (1999)*
◇ *know the truth*
⬠ *failure*
▭ *peace*

Dr. Leib Schwartzman discovered that a dialog mode exists in the Torah Code. In other words, a question is encoded in close proximity to its answer. Many of Dr. Schwartzman's discoveries utilize the dialog mode. Dr. Schwartzman was kind to let me know that the question *when will bitter come*, מתי בא מר, or, in other words, *when will bad times come*, is encoded in the Torah in skip -2. This question is encoded in one line, as a continuation to the name *Barak*. The three-letter abbreviation of the title *Prime Minister* is written in text, next to the name *Barak*. Later I noticed that the question *when will bad times come* coincides with the year *5760* (2000) or 5765 (September 2004 to September 2005). One way or another, according to the Torah Code, it appears that bad times are scheduled for when Prime Minister Barak is in power. It is significant that the year is encoded here in skip 63, the same skip which foretold the election of Ehud Barak to the post of Prime Minister.

```
גשימאשרלאברהמנתנאברהממתנתו
עליצחקבנורבעודנורחיקדמהאלארצ
הימישניחייאברהםמאשרחיימאתשנה
שנהוחמששנהימוריגועורימתאברהמב
בהזקנורשבעורימפשאלעמיורויקברו
קורישמעאלבניואלמערתהמכפלהאל
נבנצהרהחתיאשרעלפניממראהשדה
אברהמאתבניחתשמקבראברהמןש
ורהיאחרימותאברהמויברכאלהים
בנורישביצחקעמבארלחירארואלה
מעאלבנאבותהמאשרילדההגרהמצרי
רהלאברהמואלהשמותבניישמעאלב
ולדתמבכרישמעאלנביתוקדראדב
```

□ *when will bad times come*
⬠ *Barak*
▭ *abbreviation of 'Prime Minister'*
○ *5760/5765 (2000/2005)*

The term *End of Days* in Aramaic, קץ הימין, in skip -7551, coincides with *the latter days*, אחרית הימים, or *End of Days* in Hebrew, which is written in plain text in the Torah four times. In close proximity we see one of the two appearances of the name *Arafat* in skip 1 in the Torah. The name *Arafat* appears in skip 1 in the verse *for you are a stiffneckedly people*, which is written only twice in the Torah. The name *E. Barak* coincides with *End of Days*. The year *760* (2000) and *762* (2002) are encoded in one line, together with the word *year* in plain text. The underlined verse summarizes the current political situation in Israel and the peace process: *When you are in tribulation, and all these things come upon you in the latter days*.

```
תחלבוממנורנחשמבללוימכתבואתגרנוכתבואתיקבואכלתמאתובכלמ
ומגבעותהאשורנרהנעמלבדדישכונרבגורימלאיתחשמבמימנהעפריעקבו
נישנהתמיממורשניעשרנמסלתמנחהבלולרהבשמנרנסכועלתמשבתבשבת
נייההואחרתשבורהיהתמנקימנימיהוהומישראלוהיתההארצהזאתלכ
חאתראשישבטיכמאנשחכמימורדעימואתנאותמראשימעלימכמשרא
בצרלכומצאותאוככלהדבואמהאלהבאחריתהימימושבתתעדיהואלהיכוש
הארצהטורבההההזאתלרשתהכיעמקשהערפאתהזכראלתשכחאתהאשרהקצפתא
והאלהיכההמוציאכמאיצמצרימעבדימוכלישראלישמעורויראונ
האלהולאישפכדמנקירקראבאצכאשריהוהאלהיכנכנתנלכנחלהוהיהעל
לאחפצתילקחתהונגשהיקבמתואליולעינכיניהזקנימורחלצהנעלומעלרג
מזהואיהילכלאלהימכאשרדברלכוכאשרנשבעלאבתיכלאברהמליצח
```

○ *end of days*   ⬠ *Arafat*   ▭ *E. Barak*

◇ *760 (2000)*   □ *762 (2002)*   ⬡ *year*

___ *when you are in tribulation, and all these things come upon you in the latter days*

The second-minimal skip, 325, of the term *Judgment Day* is also encoded in relation to the coming holocaust. It is significant that the three minimal appearances of *Judgment Day* are connected to this setting. The minimal of the expression *Judgment Day*, in skip -39, coincides with *the judgment of the Lights before the Lord*. The third-minimal encoding of the term *Judgment Day*, in skip -627, falls together in gematria as well as in one matrix with *nuclear holocaust* and *Lights*. In the following matrix, *Judgment Day* is encoded in close proximity to *when will bad times come*, the name *Barak*, and the three-letter abbreviation of the title *Prime Minister*.

```
יפניתיהביתותומקומלגמלימויבאהאישהביתהויפתחההגמלימויתנתבנו
ביתאביתלכואלמשפחתירולקחתאשהלבניואמראלאדניאליאלתלכהאשהא
תהולגמלגמלכבאשאבהואהאשהאשרהכיחיהיהוהלבנאדניאניטראמאכלהלדב
כמעשימחסהאמתאתאדניהגידליואמלאהגידליואפנהעלימינאועל
עראתנרימימאועשורארתחרתלכויאמראלהמאלתאחרואתירויההצלחדר
איושבבבארצאגבוריצאיצחקלשובחבשרהדלפגנותערבויושאעינידוירראותהן
וחוריקשניכלאתנשבאואתדדנובנידדנהיראשורמולטושמולאמימובנים
תיאשרעלפנכממראהשדהאשרקנהאברהמאתברמחתשמניחתאברהמשרהא
נהושלשימשהושבעשניימויגועוימתויאספאלעמיוישכנומחוילהעד
לאמיממעיכיפרדוולאממלאמיאמצורביעבדצעירירימלאוירימיהלללדתו
יעיפאנכיעלכינקראשמואדומויאמריעקבמכרהכיומאתבכרתכלירימאמר
```

○ judgment day
□ when will bad times come
⬠ Barak
▭ abbreviation of 'Prime Minister'

Before writing the Torah, God scanned the blueprint while paying special attention to the post-Daniel period, for He knew that He would no longer have a person through whom to convey messages. God implemented in His blueprint a few dreadful events in case Jewish people would not abide by the covenant. However, at the beginning of Age of Aquarius, when the State of Israel would be established and developed, if this situation were to ensue, He would bring the Judgment Day. Therefore, in His blueprint, God provided for a possibility of lights and another of destruction. The Code clearly confirms the dual possibilities, and the Bible gives us an example in the Book of Jonah. God instructed the prophet Jonah to predict the destruction of the city of Nineveh. However, when the people of Nineveh heard Jonas's prediction they repented their imprudent acts and went on to live in accordance with the Torah. As a result, God was merciful and did not bring destruction on the city of Nineveh.

I believe that God's plan to remedy the dismal state of affairs on planet Earth was addressed on two different levels. First, He decided to encode the Torah, knowing that at the beginning of the Age of Aquarius people would have computers and therefore, would be able to access encoded information. Second, He decided to create a knowledge base which was to be, at the beginning, part of the oral Torah. This knowledge base was to be secretive and to be shared only by a few individuals in each generation. This knowledge base was to be called Kabbalah, and the Torah Code was to be an integral part of it. The returning souls of Jewish sages, this time as Code researchers, was the first part of His plan. It is possible that a second part had to do with God interfering in our lives once more via a living person. Kabbalah was to contain facts about the world of souls, about secrets of life, as well as to address the issue of an individual who would appear at the beginning of the Age of Aquarius, an ordinary, simple human being who would be recognized as a messenger. This messenger is called Messiah. The Book of *Zohar* addresses this issue. For generations, Kabbalah was kept as secret as possible. The Book of *Zohar* instructs Kabbalists to disseminate information at the beginning of the Age of Aquarius, the time when this messenger was scheduled to appear. Kabbalah was secretive for a long time because, first, there was no need for the public at large to know about this issue, and second, God did not want people to expect him too early, nor to invent a Messiah on their own.

Dr. Leib Schwartzman brought to my attention that in the Book of Numbers is encoded in skip -13 the phrase *the holocaust is really coming*, השואה ממש באה. This phrase is encoded only once in the Torah.

```
נ י ב נ י מ נ ל מ ש פ ח ת
מ ו פ ק ד י ה מ ח מ מ ש ה ו
א ר ב ע י מ א ל פ ו ש ש מ
א ו ת א ל ה ב נ י ד נ ל מ
ש פ ח ת ת מ ל ו ח מ מ ש פ
ח ת ה ש ו ת מ י א ל ה מ ש
פ ח ת ד נ ל מ מ ש פ ח ת מ כ
ל מ ש פ ח ת ה ש ו ח מ י ל
פ ק ד י ה מ א ר ב ע ה ו ש
ש י מ א ל פ ו א ר ב ע מ א
ו ת ב נ י א ש ר ל מ ש פ ח
ת מ ל י מ נ נ ה מ ש פ ח ת ה
י מ נ ה ל י ש ו י מ ש פ ח
```

○ *the holocaust is really coming*

I noticed that the phrase *the holocaust is really coming* (due to the length of the phrase, only part of it can be seen) coincides with the consequence of the coming holocaust – *without form and void*, תהו ובהו. This term describes the state of the world at the time of creation. The Book of Genesis tells us that *In the beginning God created the heavens and the earth. And the earth was without form and void.*

```
ל ה ו נ נ ה ה ח ג ל ה מ ל כ ה ו ת ר ת א ה ה ל מ ש פ ח ת מ נ ש ה ו פ ק ד י ה מ ש נ י מ ו ח מ ש י מ א ל פ ו ש
מ ש מ א ו ת א ל ה ב נ י י י ו ס פ ל מ ש פ ח ת מ ב נ י ר ב נ י מ נ ל מ ש פ ח ת מ ל ב ל ע מ ש פ ח ת ה ב ל ע י ל
ה מ ח מ מ ש ה ו א ר ב ע י מ א ל פ ו ש ש מ א ו ת א ל ה ב נ י ד נ ל מ ש פ ח ת מ ל ש ו ח מ מ ש פ ח ת ה ש ו ח מ
מ ש פ ח ת ה ח ב ר י ל מ ל כ י א ל מ ש פ ח ת מ ל כ י א ל י ו ש מ ב ת א ש ר ש ר ח א ל ה מ ש פ ח ת ה ב נ י א
מ ח מ ש ה ו א ר ב ע י מ א ל פ ו א ר ב ע מ א ו ת א ל ה פ ק ו ד י ב נ י י י ש ר א ל ש ש מ א ו ת א ל פ ו א ל פ
י נ ח ל ו ע ל פ י ה ג ו ר ל ת ח ל ק נ ח ל ת ה ב י נ ר ב ל מ ע ט ו א ל ה פ ק ו ד י ה ל ו י ל מ ש פ ח ת מ ל
כ ב ד ב ת ל ו י א ש ר י ל ד ה א ת ה ל ל ו י ב מ צ ר י מ ו ת ל ד ל ע מ ר מ א ת א ה ר נ ו א ת מ ש ה ו א ת מ
כ ב נ י י ש ר א ל כ י ל א נ ת נ ל ה מ נ ח ל ה ב ת ו כ ב נ י י ש ר א ל א ל ה פ ק ו ד י ד י מ ש ה ו א ל ע ז ר ה
כ י א מ כ ל ב ב נ י פ נ ה ו י ה ו ש ע ב נ נ ו נ ו ת ק ר ב נ ה ב נ ו ת צ ל פ ח ד ב נ ח פ ר ב נ ג ל ע ד ב נ
ו ה ו א ל א ה י ה ב ת ו כ ה ע ד ה ה נ ו ע ד י מ ע ל י ה ו ה ב ע ד ת ק ר ח כ י ב ח ט א ו מ ת ו ר ב נ י מ ל א
ב ת ו כ א ח י א ב י ה מ ו ה ע ב ר ת א ת נ ח ל ת א ב י ה נ ל ה נ ו א ל ב נ י י ש ר א ל ת ד ב ר ל א מ ר א י
```

○ *without form and void*   □ *the holocaust is really coming*

In this matrix you can see the term *second holocaust*, שואה שניה, in its minimal skip in the Torah, -1779. Crossing *second holocaust* is written in three consecutive lines *I am sending*, *has sent*, and *he will send*. The year *5760* or *5761* (2000 or 2001) are encoded in close proximity. Coinciding with *second holocaust* is written (in two consecutive lines) *end of Israel*. One line above it is written *the people of Israel will be slaughtered by the Arabs* (my translation), and the word *war* is encoded in skip 2. It is significant that adding the gematria of the term *second holocaust*, 677, to the gematria of the term *Judgment Day*, 125, we get 802 which is the gematria of the phrase *vengeance the covenant*, נקם ברית. From this matrix we learn that God will launch a second holocaust in the year 5761.

```
שדההמכפלהאשרעלפניממראבארצכנענאשרקנהאברהמאתהשדהמאתעפ
יוזוכלהדזורההההואובנייישראלפרוירצווירבוירבוירצמובמאדמאדות
מצריהצילךזיומידהרעימזדהלהדלהלנזווישקאתה{צ}אנוזיאמראלבנתי
ורריקמושאלהאשהמשכנתהזומזרתביתהכליכספזוכליזזהבזושמלתושמחתמ
רואלפרעהכהאמריה{ה}אלהיזיישראלשלחא{ת}עמיזויחגלייבמדברויאמר
לפרעהמלכמצרימ{י}{ת}{ו}{ד}אתבניזישראלמארצוזיידברמשהלפנייהוהלא
האלהיהעברזי{משלחנ}{ו}אליכלאמו{ש}לחאתעמיזויעבדניזיבמדברזוהנהלאש
משלחאתעמעמיזה{נ}נימשליחבכזיובעבדיכוובעמכוובבתיכאתהערבזומלאובת
בריהזומעבדזיפרעה{ה}נ{י}{ס}אתהעבדיזיואתמקנהזוהאלהבתימזואשרלאשמלב
שאאתהארבההזוי{על}{ת}בהעלכלארצמצרימויזונחבכלגבולמצרימכברדמא
לחדשהזהזוושחטו{א}תוכלקהלעדתישראלביזנהערביזמ{ו}ל{ק}{ח}{ו}{מ}{ה}{ד}מזונתנ
שכממובבנ{ישראל}{ע}זוכדברמשהזויישאלוממצרימכליכספזוכליזזהבזושמ
המדבריזמ{ס}{ו}פ{ר}חמשימעלובנייישראלמארצמצרימוזיקחמשהאתעצמותי
שזוזריטמטשהאתידועלהיהימזוישבהימלפנזותבקרלאיתנזומצרימנסימל
יתאתכלהקהלהלהזהברעבויאמריההואהאלמשהההנניממטירלכמלחממנהשמ
```

○ *second holocaust*
◇ *5760/5761 (2000/2001)*
☐☐ *end of Israel*
⬠ *he will send*
⌞⌟ *I an sending*
⌐ *has sent me*
☐ *war*

___ *the people of Israel will be slaughtered by the Arabs*

The concepts of *destruction*, *End of Days* and *Lights*, מאורות, in skip -207, come together in the following matrix. The small gematria of the number 207 is 9, which is also the small gematria of the Hebrew word light. This matrix clearly shows the two possible outcomes. The encoded word *destroyed*, השמדה, crosses the word *destruction* in plain text in the phrase *you shall not prolong your days upon it, but shall utterly be destroyed*. One line below, the word *destruction* crosses the phrase *in the End of Days*. Another verse which is written in close proximity to the encoded word *destruction* reads *for the Lord your God is a devouring fire, a jealous God*. A few meaningful phrases cross the encoded word *Lights*: *Keep the commandments of the Lord your God,* and *to teach you statutes and judgments*. Hence, looming on the horizon are two possibilities. One has to do with Lights, the other with destruction.

```
י נ י כ כ י ל א ת ה ע ב ר א ת ה י ר ד נ ה ז ה ו צ ו א ת י ה ו ש ע ו ח ז ק ה ו ו א מ צ ה ו כ י י ה ו א י ע ב
ס פ ו ע ל ה ד ב ר א ש ר א נ כ י מ צ ו ה א ת כ מ ו ל א ת כ ר ע ו מ מ נ ו ל ש מ ר א ת מ צ ו ת י ה ו ה א ל
צ ו נ י י ה ו ה א ל ה י ל ע ש ו ת כ נ ב ק ר ב ה א ר צ א ש ר א ת מ ב א י מ ש ה ל ר ש ת ה ו ש מ ר ת מ ו
מ ו מ ש פ ט י מ צ ד י ק מ כ כ ל ה ת ו ר ה ה ז א ת א ש ר א נ כ י נ ת נ ל פ נ י כ מ ה י ו מ ר ק ה ש מ ר ל
א ת י כ ל ה י מ י מ א ש ר ה מ ח י י מ ע ל ה א ד מ ה ו א ת ב נ י ה מ י ל מ ד ו נ ו ת ק ר ב ו נ ו ת ע מ ד
י מ ו א ת י צ ו ה י ה ו ה ב ע ת ה ה ו א ל ל מ ד א ת כ מ ח ק י מ ו מ ש פ ט י מ ל ע ש ת כ מ ב א ר צ
פ א ש ר ת ע ו פ ב ש מ י מ ת ב נ י ת כ ל ר מ ש ב א ד מ ה ו ת ב נ י ת כ ל ד ג ה א ש ר ב מ י מ מ ת ח ת ל א ר
ל ו ל ע מ נ ח ל ה כ י ו מ ה ז ה י ה י ה ה ת א נ כ פ נ ע ל ד ב ר י כ מ ו י ש ב ע ל ב ל ת י ע ב ר י א ת
מ פ ס ל ת מ ו נ ת כ ל א ש ר צ ו כ י ה ו ה א ל ה י כ כ י י ה ו ה א ל ה י כ א ש א כ ל ה ה ו א א ל ק נ א ב
ל א ת א ר י כ כ נ י מ ע ל י ה כ י ה ש מ ד ת ש מ ד ו נ ו ה פ י צ י ה ו ה א ת כ מ ב ב ע מ י מ ו נ ש א ר ת
כ ל ה ד ב ר י מ ה א ל ה ב א ח ר י ת ה י מ י מ ו ש ב ת ע ד י ה ו ה א ל ה י כ ו ש מ ע ת ב ק ל ו כ י א ל ר
מ ע כ מ ה ו ה ש מ ע ע מ ע מ ק ו ל א ל ה י מ מ ד ב ר מ ת ו כ ה א ש כ א ש ר ש מ ע ת א ה א ת ה ו י ח י א ו ה נ ס ה
מ י מ ה ש מ י ע כ א ת ק ל ו ל י ס ר כ ו ע ל ה א ר צ ה ר א ה צ ה ר א כ א ת א ש ו ה ג ד ל ה ו ד ב ר י ו ש מ ע ת מ
ש מ י מ מ מ ע ל ו ע ל ה א ר צ מ ת ח ת א י נ ע ו ד ו ש מ ר ת א ת ח ק י ו ו א ת מ צ ו ת י ו ו א ש ר א נ כ י
```

○ *Lights*

□ *destruction*

▭ *you shall not prolong your days upon it, but shall be utterly destroyed*

⌐▭ *for the Lord your God is a devouring fire, a jealous God*

__ *in the end of days*

⌊__⌋ *keep the commandments of the Lord your God*

- - - *to teach you statutes and judgments*

In the following matrix the term *End of Days* coincides with the encoded phrase *signs of the zodiac and a wall*, מזלות וחומה, in its minimal skip, 141. The verse which crosses the latter corresponds to the world of astronomy and maybe serves as a hint to the planetary alignment of May 10, 2000: *From one end of heaven to the other* (like a wall). One line below this phrase is written the word *in war* and under this word we see the phrase *his great fire*. Just below this configuration is encoded the words *names of God* in skip 139. A line which crosses this word reads *You shall not take the name of the Lord your God in vain.*

```
הוהאתכמשמהועבדתמשמאלהיממעשהידיאדמעצואבנאשרלאירא
מהאלהבאחריתהימימישבתעדיהוהאלהיכושמעתבבקלוכיאלרחו
אאלהימאדמעלהארצולמקצהשמימועדקצהשמימהנהיהכדברה
אתנבומופתימובמזלחמהורביידחזקהובזרועטויהובמראימגד
סרכועלהארצהראבאתאשוהגדולהיהודבריושמעתמתוכהאשותחתכ
רצמנחלהכיומהזהוידעתהיומהשבתאללבבככייהוההואהאלה
מימעלהאדמהאשריהוהאלהיכנתלכלכלהיממאזיבדילמשהשלש
צרבמדברבבארצהמישראלרלראובניאתראמתמבגלעדלגדיואתגולנב
רדנבגיאמולביתפעורובארצסחמכהאמריאשרישבבחשבונא
רעלשפתנחלארננועדהרשיאנתראחרמונוכלהערבהעברהירדנמ
היומולמדתמאתמושמרתמלעשתמיהוהאלהיכינוכרתעמנוברתבח
דביניהוהוביניכמבעתהההאלהויגידלכמאתדבריהוהכירראתמממ
סלכלתמונהאשרבשמימממעלואשרבארצמתחתואשרבמימחתלא
ביולשמרימצותולאתשאאתשמיהוהאלהיכלשואכילאינקהיהוה
להיכלאתעשהכלמלאכהאתהובנכובתכועבדכואמתכושורכוחמר
```

○ *signs of the zodiac and a wall*

— *from one end of heaven to the other*

□ *in the end of days*

⌂ *in war*

⌐⌐ *his great fire* .

□ *names of God*

⌐⌐ *you shall not take the name of the Lord your God in vain*

At this time, it seems that God has four possible options. The first one is to leave things as they are and let the process of entropy, inevitable social decline, to slowly degenerate this planet. Although this option is compatible with God's diminishing intervention in our lives, it is incompatible with Kabbalah, and incompatible with the Torah and with the prophets. In other words, this option is incompatible with God's philosophy concerning End of Days.

The second option involves returning to a period of open miracles. The long absence of God performing open miracles or interfering via a living person has produced a society which finds the Bible to be outdated and irrelevant, events to be random and God to be too abstract to believe in. The option of open miracles is a peaceful one, but 3,313 years ago, following the Exodus from Egypt, God discovered that miracles are effective only in the short term. As such, a period of open miracles by itself seems not to be a viable option.

A third option has to do with a major calamity which will destroy the vast majority of the world population. The few who will survive will start a new civilization. It is possible that this time the vehicle will not be based on religion, at least not in the form we know it. As religion has been the source of so many conflicts and wars throughout the history of mankind, it is also possible that the new order will command the survivors to preserve only one religion. God will appear once more by performing open miracles and probably by communicating via a living person. He will then establish a new order which will bring a millennium of peace and harmony. That a great calamity awaits us in the End of Days has been known for centuries. The Book of *Zohar* is explicit on this subject.

The fourth option has to do with a mixture of partial destruction and a long period of economic holocaust. It is clear that this time God's lesson is going to affect the whole world, not only Jewish people. Terms like salvation or redemption are not to be taken literally. To describe this scenario in short, the coming nuclear holocaust in the Middle East will first send stock markets into a tailspin worldwide. As a result of multinational corporations being interwoven in a global net, legal bottlenecks will further paralyze economic activities. The world will sink into stagnation and later into depression, accompanied by local violent conflicts. Under such circumstances, China may take the opportunity to realize its long-term dream to seize Taiwan, an act which will accelerate the crippling process of economic activity in the West. We may witness a civil war in Russia and in some of the other ex-soviet countries. The situation between India and Pakistan may explode, and a few other regional conflicts, like the one in Mexico, will heat up in different parts of the world. The economic situation will worsen further, especially in the US. The collapse of American stock markets in conjunction with lack of social justice in the US will bring a large segment of the population to demand a just distribution of resources and services. As US inhabitants have the right to bear arms, within a few years, the depression will transform into unbearable violence. The situation in the US will become catastrophic, and we will probably witness the first democracy to fall apart. Under such circumstances, borders will be erected again in Europe, in a desperate effort by each country to protect its citizens. In addition, there will be no money allocated to prevent AIDS and other deadly viruses from spreading, and the populations in Africa and in Asia will attenuate significantly. The world will sink further into depression and the monetary system will collapse. This time, God's lesson will be felt worldwide, precisely where people hold sacred, that is, their money. There will come a point in time when countries are too weak to embark on military activity. People will organize their lives in small communities by establishing self-sufficiency via commerce by barter. From this low point people will start realizing that society can only survive on solidarity and by sharing resources and services. The ones who survive this trough will understand that they need to love their neighbours as they love themselves in order for cohabitation to exist. Thereafter, a steady process of economic growth will ensue. This process will be slow; it will last more than a hundred years, but eventually, a better, peaceful world will enter the seventh millennium. In the end, there will be salvation, for a few, in a distant future.

The purpose of this book is to raise awareness of the inevitable Judgment Day occurring in the near future. We have been living in an era similar to the period of Judges, when society lacked leadership and decadence of moral values was the order of the day. It is apparent that God is terribly upset and disappointed. Since giving the Torah to His chosen people, God has given ample warnings and numerous harsh lessons, to no avail. Under such circumstances, it is inconceivable that God had encoded the three minimal appearances of the term *Judgment Day* to coincide with the words *nuclear holocaust, Lights, the judgment of the Lights before the Lord*, and the question *when will bad times come*, without Him carrying out Judgment Day in real life. Similarly, it is unimaginable that God would encode the term *vengeance for the covenant* to coincide with the verse *execute vengeance for the covenant*, as well as encode the expression *the Lord avenged* to coincide with *I will take vengeance* and *break my covenant*, without Him avenging the covenant.

Prime Minister Ehud Barak's "secular revolution" will complete the secular hegemony which has presided over Israel since the days of Israel's first Prime Minister, David Ben-Gurion. Furthermore, surrendering Temple Mount to the Palestinians will be detrimental to the future of Israel. The term *Eretz Israel* (the country of Israel) is not only a geographical location on planet Earth. There is also a heavenly *Eretz Israel*, one in the spiritual world. Hence, Temple Mount is not only where the First and Second Temples were situated. It is also a vital energy centre to Judaism. For Jewish people to transfer sovereignty of Temple Mount is therefore an invitation to a second holocaust. Possibly, it is Barak's "democratic, modern, advanced society," materialistically affluent and spiritually bankrupt, that finally brought the Lights to decide to implement Judgment Day. Thus, the Torah Code reveals the permanent truth of our impermanent civilization. According to the Torah Code, Judgment Day may come about in the years 5760/5761 (between September 1999 and September 2001) or in 5765/5766 (between September 2004 and September 2006). God's blueprint provides us with a few possible dates, making it impossible to accurately predict when Judgment Day will occur. Nonetheless, when Judgment Day befalls, we will know that the nuclear threat is not a phantom menace but a reality, and this reality will change the history of mankind on planet Earth.

Chapter 2
About the Psychology of Money

I used to trade financial markets and analyze price charts. As price represents the aggregate expectations of all market participants at a certain moment, one ends up studying human behaviour. It comes as no surprise that a price chart represents the hopes, fears and greed of people who trade financial markets. Not surprisingly, the term *love of money*, אהבת ממון, in its minimal appearance in the Torah, in skip -1583, coincides with verses from the Book of Leviticus, which have to do with money matters, with keeping the precepts. The following lines crossing the words *love of money*: *Take no interest from him, or increase ... that a man shall devote to the Lord of all that he has, both of man and beast, and of the field of his possession, shall be sold or redeemed.*

```
והואבדלאתכממנהעמימלהיותליואישואשהכייהיהבהמאובאוידענ
אנייהוהושמראתמשמרתיולאישאועליוחטאומתוובכייחללהואנויי
לואמרתאלהמכיתבאואלהארצאשראנינתנלכמוקצרתמאתקצירהוהבאת
בדכלנדריכמומלבדכלכלנדבתיכמאשרתתנניליהוהאכבחממשהעשריומלחד
וניהיהלארצשבתהליהוהשדכלאתרעוכרתמלאתזמראתסכפיחקצירכלאת
כומטהידודעמכיוהחזקתביוגרותושביוחיישעמאלתקחמאתונשכותרביתרי
אולכאתכמכמקומיותואמלאתמשמעוליולאתעשואתכלהמצותהאלהואמבח
ואתחקקתיגעלהנגפשמיואפגמזאתהבהיותמהיארצאירביהמלאמאסתימולאנ
שריחרמאישליהוהמכלאשרלומאדמובהמהומשדהאחזתולאימכרולאיג
אפקדיהמלמלמטהזבולנשבעהוחמשיןמאלפיארבעמאותלבנייוספלבבניואפ
ורבנשדיאורוצבאוופקדיושהוארבעיומאלפיוחמשמאותותהחזונמעלי
ישראלוהיוליהלויוימכילייכלבכורבריומהכתיכלבכורברבארצמצרימהקד
```

○ *love of money*
▭ *take no interest from him, or increase*
__ *that a man shall devote to the Lord of all that he has, both of man and beast, and of the field of his possession, shall be sold or redeemed*

Had Gertrude Stein read Karl Marx and Sigmund Freud, she probably would not have written during the summer of 1936 in the *Saturday Evening Post* that money was funny, nor that "money is money and that is all there is about it." Both Marx and Freud have shown that there is plenty more to money, and it is far from being funny.

From a purely theoretical point of view, in economics, money is any circulating medium of exchange, means of payment, unit of account, measure of wealth or standard of value. In his *Philosophy of Right* (1967), Hegel demonstrates that money is a universal medium of exchange which actualizes the abstract value of all commodities – abstract, because once we depart from a world of barter to use paper money, a bill does not represent the paper it is printed on; rather, it is a symbol of value.

Let us see first what money does to people and what people do to money. According to Karl Marx, money has not only a given reality in bourgeois society but also a psychological role in the relationship between people in an economic setup. Marx's great accomplishment is to characterize money in the context of social interactions, for, beyond the economic theory, the value of money is related to the value of the individual and to general human values (Rendon, 1991). In *Economic and Philosophic Manuscripts of 1844* (1987), Marx notes that

> By possessing the property of buying everything, by possessing the property of appropriating all objects, money is thus the object of eminent possession. The universality of its property is the omnipotence of its being. It therefore functions as the almighty being…. That which is for me through the medium of money – that for which I can pay (i.e., which money can buy) – that am I, the possessor of the money.

Furthermore, continues Marx, money has the ability to transform human incapacity and human characteristics. To demonstrate this capacity of money, Marx quotes from Shakespeare's play *The Life of Timon of Athens*. Lord Timon of Athens was extremely altruistic and charitable while he was wealthy. As a result of this generosity, he lost all he had. To his bewilderment, despite all the help he had given the people of Athens in earlier years, they betrayed him. No one was willing to lend him even the smallest amount of money nor to support him. Full of bitterness, he went to live in a cave and became an adversary to mankind in general and Athens in particular. Timon's tragedy best portrays the role money plays in human relationships. To show that money is the root of all evil, Marx further quotes from the Antigone of Sophocles:

> Nothing so evil as money ever grew to be current among men. This lays cities low, this drives men from their homes, this trains and warps honest souls till they set themselves to works of shames; this still teaches folk to practise villainies, and to know every godless deed.

As the object of eminent possession, as the goal of all desires, money becomes the mediator between commodities and services, between buyers and sellers whose sole interest is the mediator itself, since "the only force bringing them together, and putting them into relation with each other, is the selfishness, the gain and the private interest of each. Each pays heed to himself only, and no one worries about the others" (Marx, 1987). Hence, money not only binds people; it alienates people. Thus it serves at the same time as the universal agent of separation and divorce.

Another decisive quality of money is derived from its utilization as the universal medium of exchange. By serving as a measure of value for all commodities, products and services, money is converted to a common denominator which in turn, reduces everything to its abstract form. It strips everything it measures of its intrinsic value. "[Money] robs everything and every person of individuality and thereby debases what it touches" (Dimen, 1994). For Marx, money is an alienable commodity "because it is all other commodities divested of their shape... money is independent of all limits... because it is directly convertible into any other commodity" (Marx, 1990).

Consequently, money is the active concept of value; value depends on need, and need provokes emotions. Money is the only medium in the world that (depending on the quantity one possesses) provides at the same time comfort, freedom and power. Precisely for that reason money takes on an emotional value. Money managers, investors, traders and speculators assert that when a person's equity starts fluctuating, so do his emotions. As Hallowell and Grace put it, "The emotional meaning of money to any one person may have roots that twist and turn through the past and the unconscious as circuitously and mysteriously as any other deeply felt issue… Most people have a rich and complex set of associations to money, full of displaced meaning, rife with the most intense affects, and guarded by a host of dogged defenses" (Hallowell and Grace, 1991). Similarly, Mario Rendon, professor of clinical psychiatry at New York Medical College and editor of the *American Journal of Psychoanalysis*, writes that "The power of money over man is a magic that remains – perhaps wittingly – untouched. There is no more powerful reinforcer and no more universal narcotic than money" (Rendon, 1991). And according to David Krueger, "Money is probably the most emotionally meaningful object in contemporary life; only food and sex are its close competitors as common carriers of such strong and diverse feelings, significances, and strivings" (Krueger 1986).

I find it surprising that Sigmund Freud did not write extensively about money. One would have expected the inventor of psychoanalysis, who investigated and wrote at length about sexual anxiety and sexual frustration, to elucidate as well the passion for money, or maybe money neuroses. On one hand he observes that "money is to be regarded in the first instance as a medium for self preservation and for obtaining power," but, on the other hand, "powerful sexual factors are involved in the value set upon it." In his paper "On Beginning the Treatment," Freud instructs psychoanalysts concerning their fees. He points out that "money questions will be treated by cultured people in the same manner as sexual matters, with the same inconsistency, prudishness, and hypocrisy" (Freud, 1995). Similar observations are reported by several psychoanalysts, for example, Josef Weissberg (1991) who notices that people would rather discuss their sexuality and fantasies than their financial situation. By the same token, Sheila Klebanow (1991) notes that money is "too private, too intimate, its personal details far too revealing" for people to talk about.

One can only hypothesize in an attempt to find an explanation as to why Freud does not pay more attention to the subject of money. Ernest Jones writes in *The Life and Work of Sigmund Freud* (1993) that money had no emotional significance for Freud and that his attitude toward it was markedly normal. In his day, "Viennese parents would never even discuss their income with their children; it was a forbidden topic which had to be avoided" (Warner, 1991). This was the education Freud received at home, and this was the philosophy he adopted for his own children. Jones describes how lenient, free and friendly father Freud was to his children. He wanted them to have everything they wanted for their pleasure and education. "In the meantime the children were not only not to have any anxiety about money, but even to know as little as possible about it – nothing in fact beyond their own little allowances." Unquestionably, Freud's financial situation during the last quarter of the nineteenth century and the first twenty years of this century was difficult. In "An Autobiographical Study," he writes that his family "lived in very limited circumstances," and in 1882, a year after he graduated as a medical doctor, he took his teacher's advice to abandon his theoretical career and enter the General Hospital as a clinical assistant "in view of my bad financial position." In Paris, in 1885, he had very little money and was living on loans. Back in Vienna in 1886, "there were times when he could not afford to take a cab to make house calls" (Gay, 1987), and he was constantly afraid of not being able to provide for his family. Later, on April 20, 1895, he writes to Wilhelm Fliess, "I cannot accept your proposal to come to Berlin now. My circumstances are such that I cannot allow myself to spend 1,000 to 1,500 florins, or even half that amount, on my own health." And in another letter, dated September 21, 1899: "My mood also depends very strongly on my earnings. Money is laughing gas for me…. Thus I came to know the helplessness of poverty and continually fear it. You will see that my style will improve and my ideas will be more correct if this city provides me with an ample livelihood" (Masson, 1985). As a result, a few close friends of Freud supported him financially for years. That monetary support became a source of ambivalence and frustration as, on the one hand, Freud felt he was entitled to receive the money, while on the other, he resented being indebted to them (Warner, 1991). Due to these financial arrangements, his relationship with his colleague and benefactor, Josef Breuer, turned sour. "Our intimate friendship later gave place to a total estrangement; –money played a great part among the reasons for my estrangement" (Freud, 1991). After World War I, he found himself close to bankruptcy. Apart from having fewer patients, inflation was eroding his savings.

To the best of my knowledge, Freud first expressed in writing his feelings towards money in a letter written to Wilhelm Fliess on December 22, 1897 (Masson, 1985):

> I can scarcely detail for you all the things that resolve themselves into – excrement for me (a new Midas!). It fits in completely with the theory of internal stinking. Above all, money itself. I believe this proceeds via the word "dirty" for "misery."… This is really wild, but it is entirely analogous to the process by which words take on a transferred meaning as soon as new concepts requiring a designation appear.

The connection between money and feces is significant for Freud on two very different levels: the linguistic one, which is assimilated with unconscious thinking, and the physical one, for which he seeks a scientific explanation. Let us first focus on the linguistic plane. What is the source for the notion "filthy rich," when we refer to a person who "keeps too careful a hold on his money," or the use of the expression "dirty money" when we refer to his equity? For Freud, the source hides in a deeper level, as he writes in "Character and Anal Erotism" (1991):

> In reality, whatever archaic modes of thought have predominated or persisted – in the ancient civilizations, in myths, fairy tales and superstitions, in unconscious thinking, in dreams and in neuroses –

money is brought into the most intimate relationship with dirt.... Thus in following the usage of language, neurosis, here as elsewhere, is taking words in their original, significant sense, and where it appears to be using a word figuratively it is usually simply restoring its old meaning. It is possible that the contrast between the most precious substance known to men and the most worthless.... has led to this specific identification of gold with faeces.

Follow me, if you will, in a digression before we get to Freud's physical solution for the connection between money and feces, for in this detour we will try to penetrate Freud's subconscious. In a letter to Wilhelm Fliess, dated January 24, 1897, Freud asked his friend to recommend him "some good reading" regarding witches and devils. "I read one day that the gold the devil gives his victims regularly turns into excrement.... In connection with the dancing in witches' confessions, remember the dance epidemics in the Middle Ages." Freud probably referred to a type of hysteria that appeared in 1374 in the form of a dancing mania. Poor people, servants, beggars, mainly unmarried women, danced in circles in the streets and churches, leaping and screaming, convinced that they were possessed by demons. "A pact with the Devil offered pleasure without penitence, enjoyment of sexuality, riches and earthy ambitions" (Tuchman, 1978). Then, in *Character and Anal Erotism* (1991), Freud suggests again that "the gold which the devil gives his paramours turns into excrement after his departure" and "even according to ancient Babylonian doctrine gold is 'the faeces of Hell'." In the Middle Ages, Christians considered business and money as evils; charging interest on a loan was equated with committing the sin of usury. "A man who is a merchant can seldom if ever please God," reads St. Jerome's dictum (Tuchman, 1978). Consequently, dealing with money and commerce constituted the "dirty work" that was left to the Jews, who were practically excluded from more respectable occupations and trades, as part of the anti-Semitic persecution mania of the Middle Ages. To mark the separation of Jews, "Innocent III in 1215 decreed the wearing of a badge, usually in the form of a wheel or circular patch of yellow felt, said to represent a piece of money…. A hat with a point rather like a horn, said to represent the Devil, was later added further to distinguish the Jews." Identifying the devil's figure with the one of a tradesman was common, as prior to the fourteenth century, men "could hardly imagine the merchant's strongbox without picturing the devil squatting on the lid." (Tuchman, 1978). In fact, the Torah and the Talmud take the same attitude to usury and interest on loans. A Jew is forbidden to charge interest from a fellow Jew. In the Book of Deuteronomy 23:19 God orders His people: *You shall not lend upon interest to your brother, interest on money, interest on victuals, interest on anything that is lent for interest.* Similarly, in the Book of Leviticus 25:35,36 this obligation also applies to a Gentile needing money for his survival: *And if your brother becomes poor, and cannot maintain himself with you, you shall maintain him; as a stranger and a sojourner he shall live with you. Take no interest from him or increase, but fear your God; that your brother may live beside you. You shall not lend him your money at interest, nor give him food for profit.* The Talmud prohibits charging interest throughout, whether between Jews or non-Jews.

This is then, for Freud, the devil's gold: the anachronistic, repugnantly anti-Semitic notion of linking money to Jews and the use of the word devil in the Middle Ages to stain those Jews. The Jew is resented and despised, as his sole interaction with the society reduces itself to money and indebtedness. Although Freud considered himself an atheist, "A Godless Jew," an "old Semite," or "a shabby old Israelite" and although his identification with Judaism was aggressively secular (Gay, 1987), he was extremely sensitive to any indication of anti-Semitism. I think one can reasonably theorize that this connection in Freud's mind (money→Jew→devil) brought him to equate money to feces. During periods of indigence, shortage and financial crisis, money has the capacity to ignite anti-Semitism, to degrade a Jew because he is a Jew. That capacity that money has, says Freud, equates it to something that is worthless. It is my opinion that Freud searched for a scientific explanation to validate this equation on a physical level, the result of which manifested itself via his theory child→feces→gift→money. Freud speculates in "On Transformations of Instinct as Exemplified in Anal Erotism" (1991), that "it is probable that the first meaning which a child's interest in faeces develops is that of 'gift' rather than 'gold' or 'money'.... Since his faeces are his first gift, the child easily transfers his interest from that substance to the new one which he comes across as the most valuable gift in life."

In "A Seventeen-Century Demonological Neurosis" (1990), Freud explains that although the devil is the antithesis of God, they are very close in nature and originally were identical. "The evil demon of the Christian faith – the Devil of the Middle Ages – was, according to Christian mythology, himself a fallen angel and of a godlike nature.... In the earliest ages of religion God himself still possessed all the terrifying features which were afterwards combined to form a counterpart of him." Later in Freud's life, his analysis of the devil figure appears in a more crystallized form in "Civilization and its Discontents" (1991), in which he makes explicit the parallel between devil and Jew as scapegoat: "The devil would be the best way out as an excuse for God; in that way he would be playing the same part as an agent of economic discharge as the Jew does in the world of the Aryan ideal." Very significantly, in "Character and Anal Erotism" (1991), Freud asserts that "the devil is certainly nothing else than the personification of the repressed unconscious instinctual life."

According to Freud, if the most detested supreme spirit of evil, the devil, is close in its nature, even identical to the most cherished Supreme Being, God, why then should not the most worthless of substances, feces, be identical to the most precious of elements, gold? For Freud, gold equals feces because, in his subconscious, anti-Semitism links the Jew of the Middle Ages to the devil who is identified with whoever deals with money. In general, Freud has "not found much of the 'good' in people" (Jones, 1993), but in my opinion, the idea that provoked the greatest resentment in Freud was that Jews be treated as scapegoats. Witnessing the rise of anti-Semitism in Europe, Freud laments that "unfortunately all the massacres of the Jews in the Middle Ages did not suffice to make that period more peaceful and secure for their Christian fellows" (Freud, 1991).

Freud began his university studies in 1873, just after the peak of a golden period for Viennese Jewry. Between the years 1857 and 1880, Jewish constitutional rights improved dramatically, and the Jewish population in Vienna grew from 6,000 to 72,000. The last legal discriminations had been abolished in 1867, but then came the stock market crash of "Black Friday," on May 9, 1873, which changed the course of life in Austria. Experiencing massive capital dissipation and huge losses, the Austrians' search for a scapegoat brought anti-Semitism to centre stage. Half a century later Freud writes, in "An Autobiographical Study" (1993), about his experience during his first year at the University of Vienna:

> I found that I was expected to feel myself inferior and an alien because
> I was a Jew. I refused absolutely to do the first of these things. I have
> never been able to see why I should feel ashamed of my descent or, as
> people were beginning to say, of my 'race'. I put up, without much
> regret, with my non-acceptance into the community.

Freud graduated as a medical doctor in 1881, but his academic advance to the rank of university professor was delayed for seventeen years, possibly because of bureaucratic anti-Semitism. However, it is possible that his postulation of sexuality as the bedrock for psychoanalysis proved to be too avant-garde for nineteen century Austria and as a result, it is difficult to pinpoint the reason for the deliberate slowdown of his academic career. James Strachey, in *Sigmund Freud: A Sketch of his Life and Ideas*, strongly believes it to have been "held back by political influence."

Another interpretation of Freud's reference to the devil's gold is given in Muriel Dimen's excellent article, "Money, Love and Hate" (1994):

> Money and love, the twin engines that make the world go round, at
> least the world as we know it, do not go together at all. Worse. They
> negate, undo one another, and their contradiction funds alienation....

You now see you knew all along that what you thought was pure gold was false, that what you thought would uplift you only degrades you…. This degradation, then, is the devil's gold…. It is a gift given after passion is spent…. That capacity to make everything less than it is…. that capacity, says Freud, is what money has. That's why it's the Devil's gold.

If we follow Dimen's interpretation, then indeed, money and love contradict each other; for where there is true love, money counts little. As love intensifies, money and love disunite geometrically, reaching a point where monetary considerations do not exist. If you ever truly loved someone, you will definitely understand what I mean. The opposite brings us to reflect on the devil's gift to his lover, turns to excrement when he leaves, and evokes the situation of separation or divorce, as when love has dissipated and the only thing left is money.

Apparently, the Torah Code connects the terms *love of gold*, אהבת זהב, and *lust for sex*, תאות מין. In the following matrix we can see the minimal appearance in the Torah of the term *love of gold*, in skip -1188, coinciding with the minimal skip, 14, of the term *lust for sex*. The phrases *you shall not make your souls abominable* and *love your neighbour as yourself* are written in close proximity.

```
פרעליוהכהנלפנייהוהמזובווראישיכיתצאממנשכבתזרעורחצבמימאתכלבשרוטמאעדהערבוכלבגדוכללעורואשרי
נפתבדיצנפבנגדיקדשהםורחצבמימאתבשרוולבשמומאתנעדתבניישראליקחשניישעירריעזימלחטאתואיראחדלעלהוהוה
צאתנבשרולנמימבנקומקדושולחצשאתמגדיווייצאוועשהאתעלתוואתעלתהעמוכפרבעדודובעדהעמואחדלבהחטאתוקטיר
ואישאישמביתישראלומנהגרחבתוכמאשריאכלכלדמונתיופניובנפשהאכלאתהאתקרבענמהכינפשה
אתתנשכבתכלזרעולטמאהבהומטעכלתאתנלהעבירלמלכולזאתחללאתשמאלהיכאניייהוהוארכרלאתשכבמשכבראשתה
כולאתשאעלייוחסאלאתתקמולאאשראתהבנתלרעבכמוכאנייהוהאתחקתיתשמרובהמתכלאתרביעכלאישמשדכל
תירהמיתאתושמתייאניאאנפונגאישהדיאואובשפתחויוהכרתיאתוילדנותאחריילדןזנותאחרביעכלמשד
ולאתשקצואתנפשתיכמבהמהובעובפוכלאשרתרמשהאדמהאשרהבדלתילכמלטמאהוהיהמליקדשימכיקדושאנייהוה
כיאנייהוהמקדשמוידברמשהאלאהרנואלבניוואלכלבניישראלוידברליהוהאלמשהלאמרדבראלאהרנואלבנייווי
אשהלאתתנומהמעלהמהמזבחלייהוהישורושוהשרונותלימבדתהתאשגאתרקלטומעוכתהותונתהוקובכרותכלאת
בתמיידומהביאכמאתהעמהמרהתנגיפהשבעעשובתנ נהעדממחרתהשמביעתתסברוחמשימימיומוהקרבתמחדחד
```

○ *love of gold*

□ *lust for sex*

▭ *you shall not make your souls abominable*

⊓ *love your neighbour as yourself*

These days, values in general and social justice in particular have all but disappeared in Western societies, as the system encourages greed, selfishness and egoism. The goal of the citizen is to have and to have more. As Erich Fromm (1995) wrote, societies which do not encourage these traits of greed, selfishness and egoism are considered "primitive" and their inhabitants "childlike." Not surprisingly, the US remains the country with the most unequal income distribution among Western economies. This gap between rich and poor has been widening steadily. Setting aside Marxist doctrine and its macroeconomics philosophy, I find Marx's perception of a person's attitude toward money in capitalist societies to be as relevant, as accurate and as applicable to individual striving for money at the present time as it was in his day. More than that, such perception embraces a much broader base of our society, as the quantity of money in circulation is so much greater today than in the middle of the nineteenth century. Unfortunately, "the greatest intensity and expansion of this desire [for money] occurred in those times in which the modest satisfaction of individual life-interests… had lost its power… the whole aspect of life, the relationships of human beings with one another and with objective culture are coloured by monetary interests" (Simmel, 1991).

Interestingly enough, a recent book by Michèle Lamont, *Money, Morals & Manners* (1992), compares attitudes of the French and American upper-middle classes toward money. During a conversation with the author, a Frenchman is quoted as saying he was "irritated by people who are always looking for an edge, who think only about money, who would do everything to advance." The author adds that an important group of French respondents thought of money "as impure" and that for many Frenchmen the author talked to, money was unworthy of pursuit. Two other Frenchmen said they had "little admiration for people whose goal is to get rich." Such negative attitudes towards money as those expressed by Frenchmen are rare in the United States, where class is defined mainly by the equity one possesses. Along these lines, Lamont remarks that a "sizable number of American social and cultural specialists seem to believe that people who are really smart 'go for the money' and that only 'losers', people who are not 'totally with it', and people who could not pay for the training that would qualify them for higher-paying work, would take a job with low monetary rewards."

Probably there has not been a period in history during which individuals were not greedy. While the Roaring Twenties can serve as a recent example, the extravagant financial feast of the last twenty-five years has surpassed the wildest of imagining. The origins of this financial orgy can be explained by events that took place in the period 1971-74. Maybe the most crucial change happened in August 1971, when President Nixon abolished the gold standard, which had been in effect since the Bretton Woods Conference of 1944 and which had provided the Western world with stable economic conditions, low levels of inflation, low interest rates, fixed currency exchange rates and steady GNP growth. Nixon's action brought havoc to the monetary system and to the economic order in general, as interest rates, exchange rates and the price of gold were allowed to float freely in accord with market forces. John Eatwell, a financial specialist from Cambridge University notes that

> In 1971, just before the collapse of the Bretton Woods fixed exchange rate system, about 90 percent of all foreign exchange transactions were for the finance of trade and long-term investment, and only about ten percent were speculative. Today those percentages are reversed, with well over ninety percent of all transactions being speculative... the sheer scale of speculative flows can easily overwhelm any government's foreign-exchange reserves (Eatwell, 1993).

A year later, in 1972, adverse weather conditions wiped out the preponderance of the Soviet Union's crops. The massive US grain exports which followed caused prices to rise tremendously, creating unprecedented volatility in US grain markets. In a further development, the oil price increases during 1973-74 by OPEC countries brought an enormous expansion to capital markets and huge recycling of petrodollars into the world's financial centres. As well, in January 1974, the United States eliminated all capital controls. The stage was set for the biggest speculative spree in history.

Republican economic policies during the 1980s unleashed the ugly cravings of notoriously alienated, greedy people. "Go for it" has become the motto, legitimating the drive for selfish fulfillment. As Erich Fromm writes in *To Have Or To Be*:

> To be an egoist refers not only to my behaviour but to my character. It means: that I want everything for myself; that possessing, not sharing, gives me pleasure; that I must become greedy because if my aim is having, I *am* more the more I *have*; that I must feel antagonistic towards all others; my customers whom I want to deceive, my competitors whom I want to destroy, my workers whom I want to exploit. I can never be satisfied, because there is no end to my wishes; I must be envious of those who have more and afraid of those who have less. But I have to repress all these feelings in order to represent myself (to others as well as to myself) as the smiling, rational, sincere, kind human being everybody pretends to be (1995).

Touché. In the US, alienation has become second nature, acknowledged as a fact of life. One is required to be efficient, correct, but not required to show affection, nor to exhibit emotions, nor to care for someone who has been fired, nor to feel compassion for a fellow American. One is obliged to express only what is "politically correct," to say the right thing so the deal does not fall apart, regardless of whether one believes in what one says, regardless of whether one is telling the truth. In the milieu of Corporate America, only a fool would dare express his opinion aloud if it is not in line with the corporation's interest. Fromm defined it as a "marketing character," whose function is to achieve the most benefit for the corporation employing him; the character must always defend the organization's position. This alienation, states Fromm, is similar to posthypnotic behaviour. A person awakening from an hypnotic trance will follow orders previously given to him, without any consideration or awareness of the fact he is not doing what he really *wants* to do. On August 23, 1999, the newspaper *Globe and Mail* published an article titled "Compaq Canada Climbs the Training Wall." The computer giant has been sending its employees to a corporate training indoor 'wilderness' centre *Above & Beyond*, located in a Toronto industrial building. In this training centre, Compaq employees are instructed to traverse a 12.1-metre "toxic" river, and scale a 10.6-metre-high "rock" wall. Furthermore, they are hoisted onto a ropes course suspended six metres overhead, and required to climb a steep pole and then to jump off. The centre's founder, Andrew Levison, explains: "The stuff we do in the gym is designed not to put people at ease with each other, but to make them uncomfortable, because that's what business is all about." Evidently, this is precisely what happens when corporations come first and people come second. In this context, it will be helpful to remember that during Aristotle's times in Athens, alienating work was done only by slaves, while in our modern system, alienated workers are the type of people Corporate America is hiring. Erich Fromm further describes the marketing character:

> Success depends largely on how well they get their 'personality' across, how nice a 'package' they are; whether they are 'cheerful', 'sound', 'aggressive', 'reliable', 'ambitious'; furthermore, what their family backgrounds are, what clubs they belong to, and whether they know the 'right' people…. The aim of the marketing character is complete adaptation, so as to be desirable under all conditions of the personality market…. Since the marketing characters have no deep attachment to themselves or to others, they do not care, in any deep sense of the word, not because they are so selfish but because their relations to others and to themselves are so thin (1995).

Gerry Spence, in his perceptive and excellent book, *From Freedom to Slavery*, labeled corporate America as the New King. This ferocious New King is the emerging tyrant, the enslaving force in America. These nonliving corporate entities are

encased and protected by endless layers of governmental bureaucracies. The primary strategy of the New King is to convert all rights, all human energy, all goals and, at last, all humans into fungible commodities, for the New King exists solely for commerce and its life's blood, its green blood, its money – and its singular mission is profit (Spence, 1993).

It seems that Americans have forgotten that the Constitution was signed for their benefit, to guarantee their freedom and the pursue of their happiness; it was not signed for the welfare of corporations. One wonders how is it that the individual in the US has become so tame, so docile, as to hand the corporation his power, his freedom and his rights.

A New King was crowned when we capitulated to a regime that was no longer sensitive to people but to non-people – to corporations, to money and to power. The New King was crowned when we turned our heads as the poor and the forgotten and the damned were rendered mute and defenseless... they seemed unimportant... they were essentially powerless (Spence, 1993).

This situation has come about because an unprecedented massive complex of draconian laws has been enacted by the government. No legal system in any European democratic country comes even close to the monstrosity of the American system. And no European democracy enforces its laws in such an inhumane manner, with such arbitrariness and excessive official formality. In a recent bestseller, *The*

Death of Common Sense, Philip Howard states that "we have constructed a system of regulatory law that basically outlaws common sense. Modern law, in an effort to be 'self-executing,' has shut out our humanity… only the massive weight of accumulated laws keeps everyone in check" (Howard, 1994). How does an individual feel in this atmosphere of inhumanity and alienation? He is afraid. He is fearful of breaking the law, he is afraid of the police, of the FBI, of the IRS, of the ATF and other government agencies. Mere knowledge of being investigated by a government agency is enough to ruin a person's life because of the very fact that in the US, "we embrace the myth that we are still a democracy when we know that we are not a democracy, that we are not free, that the government does not serve us but subjugates us" (Spence, 1993).

It is interesting to gauge the level of fear in the US. The last time I was in the Museum of Science in Boston, I saw at the museum's store a machine which is called 'Owl penny machine'. The machine transforms a one-cent coin into an elliptical piece of copper with a design of an owl engraved into it. The amusing thing about this gimmick is a metal plate affixed to this machine which reads: "Yes, it's legal. US Code 18-331." You see, the US government needs to pacify a grandmother who takes her grandchild to the museum by assuring her that it is lawful to destroy her own one-cent coin! One would think that if a Science Museum, which probably belongs to the municipality of Boston, allows such a machine on its premises, then someone checked that the machine is legal. But no, no, it is not enough; in the general campaign to produce acquiescence to authorities, the municipality needs to inform the fearful citizen that by destroying her one-cent coin she is not breaking the law.

Another outrageous situation for every US resident is the possibility of being sued in a court of law. So real is the fear of being sued that only in the US would a person fainting on a sidewalk remain unassisted by other pedestrians for the fear that, later, the person who fainted would sue the person who rushed to help him, in the unlikely event that somehow the assistance hurt rather than helped him. To sue a person or better still, a corporation, seeking to gain money for whatever damage or wrongful conduct, real or imagined, has become a national sport in America. Only the wealthy can afford to hire excellent defence lawyers, so when the average guy is sued by another person or, worse, by a corporation or a government agency, his chance of winning the lawsuit is slim. Out of this fear come silence, pretence and alienation. People are afraid to say what they think, afraid to take action against a corporation or an official for fear of getting involved in litigation. As Gerry Spence says, "Freedom in America works best for those who can afford it" (Spence, 1993). This, we are told, is democracy in the land of opportunity, the United States of America, which strangely enough is always concerned about human rights in other countries.

Sigmund Freud detested the materialistic, shallow values of American culture; Karl Marx was terrified of money's power to transform and corrupt human beings. Today, more than ever before, the US is the embodiment of Marx's apprehension and Freud's loathing. The much advertised freedom of US residents has taken on the proportions of brainwashing when in reality, their freedom is dwindling to zero. An extremely complex structure of regulations and institutions has been created to provide a safety net for financial markets, banks and corporations. As necessary and as positive as this is, hardly any safety net exists for individuals. For that reason, freedom is enjoyed by financial markets, banks and corporations, but not by people. As Isaiah Berlin wrote "total liberty for wolves is death to the lambs, total liberty of the powerful, the gifted, is not compatible with the rights to a decent existence of the weak and the less gifted" (Berlin, 1990). The Dow Jones average has risen more than fourteen fold since the summer of 1982, but has this spectacular increase been reflected in the standard of living of the American worker? A recent study of the Federal Reserve indicates that, despite the go-go American stock market, the net worth of the poor has diminished. In other words, not only has the poor person not retained his position in relation to the rich or to the middle class, but his net worth has declined in absolute terms.

The question must be asked: How weak, docile and alienated are US inhabitants that they are able to accept such a situation in their own country, when tens of thousands of workers are fired for the sake of corporate profit? Or rather: How strong is the regime, how strong and immune are the corporations that they can bring this kind of calamity on their fellow Americans with impunity? In this atmosphere of alienation, in which the loyalty of citizens is to the dollar, not to their fellow citizens, one remembers Lord Timon's sentence on humanity in Shakespeare's play: "The unkindest beast more kinder than mankind." And in *Capital III*, Marx's metaphor goes even further. He cites the pamphlet, *Killing No Murder*, published in 1657, which called the assassination of Cromwell justified and appropriate, to make an analogy to the world of commerce, claiming that when profits are at stake, killing is no murder. As Noam Chomsky (1992) shows, this is not a metaphor. Killings and tortures in Third World countries were supported by the US when the rights of capitalist enterprises and investors were threatened. Money is the universal language, and the axiom everyone understands asserts that the continuation of the system depends on profits.

One of the brightest intellectuals of this century, Noam Chomsky, in his book, *What Uncle Sam Really Wants* (1992), describes a ruthless US doctrine which ties together foreign policy in the Third World and control of the domestic population. The power "basically lies in the hands of the people who determine investment decisions," stability means security for the upper class and large enterprises. The primary enemy of de facto policy makers is the domestic population. This US doctrine reinforces "the basic social values: passivity, submissiveness to authority, the overriding virtue of greed and personal gain, lack of concern for others, fear of real or imagined enemies, etc. The goal is to keep the bewildered herd bewildered" (Chomsky, 1992). Chomsky exposes the chilling nature of US policies in the Third World:

We must therefore combat a dangerous heresy which, US intelligence reported, was spreading through Latin America: "the idea that the

government has direct responsibility for the welfare of the people...."
We've consistently opposed democracy if its results can't be controlled.
The problem with real democracies is that they're likely to fall prey
to the heresy that governments should respond to the needs of their
own population, instead of those of US investors (Chomsky, 1992).

Keeping the herd bewildered and afraid is easier when people are selfish, greedy and alienated. In Chomsky's view, Cold War politics provided both the US and the former USSR with the possibility of controlling and terrifying the local populations, with each side "using the other to justify repression and violence in its own domains" (Chomsky, 1992). He goes on to posit that the end of the Cold War and the disappearance of the Evil Empire required a substitute for the government to use to terrify the population; that the surrogate conflict became the "war on drugs." Chomsky argues that "Domestically, it has little to do with drugs but a lot to do with distracting the population, increasing repression in the inner cities, and building support for the attack on civil liberties" (Chomsky, 1992).

In a letter to Ernest Jones, dated March 18, 1921, Freud states: "It is puzzling, how little '*Gemeinsinn*' [community spirit] and tendency for organization there is to be found among the better elements in America, only the robbers and pirates hunt in gangs." Again, in a letter to Jones written in the following month, Freud observes:

I think competition is much more pungent with them; not succeeding
means civil death to every one, and they have no private resources
apart from their profession, no hobby, games, love or other interests
of a cultured person. And success means money. Can an American
live in opposition to the public opinion, as we are prepared to do?
(Paskauskas, 1995).

Already at the beginning of the century Freud recognized that the New World is governed "by the dollar," that "the country and its denizens were hypocritical, uncultivated, shallow, enamored of money alone.... But worst of all, America was enslaved to that favorite product of anal adult, money" (Gay, 1987). For Freud, the anal character is a person whose anal-erotic phase remained dominant from childhood throughout his development, and therefore, as an adult, he directs his energy and goals to materialism, greed and stinginess. Erich Fromm explains that since the qualities of an anal character constitute the norm of moral behaviour, Freud's concept becomes in effect a sharp criticism of bourgeois society and its possessiveness and could be correlated to Marx's evaluation of men and money in the *Economic and Philosophical Manuscripts*. "For Freud, in other words, the person exclusively concerned with having and possession is a neurotic, mentally sick person; hence it would follow that the society in which most of the members are anal characters is a sick society" (Fromm, 1995).

The philosophy of laissez faire assumes that when market partakers have the freedom to pursue their self interest, resources will be allocated in the most efficient way. Therefore, one would have expected that in the US, which has a system of open society and competitive markets, we would encounter the highest efficiency in allocation of resources. Instead, we find poverty, homelessness and forty-three million people without medical insurance. This obviously means that the poor and the homeless are not among the concerns of markets, nor among the concerns of Corporate America. This is understandable but as a result, it becomes the obligation of the government to take care of them. As we know, the US government does not consider taking care of the poor and the homeless to be part of its ethical obligations.

When capitalism goes too far to the 'right', as it has in our world, social values are lost. In general, during the last thirty years and especially since the oil-price hikes which followed The Yom Kippur War in 1973, the amount of money in circulation expanded geometrically worldwide. As a result, the standard of living went up, especially in Western democracies. Prosperity is a significant achievement, but there is a serious problem which comes along with it: not many people are psychologically equipped to go up the ladder, to handle this kind of transformation; from being merely able to provide for their well-being, to a second level of being able to handle freedom, to a third level of being able to use power. In the same way that money has the capacity to ignite anti-Semitism in countries which go through a financial crisis, money has the capacity to ignite Machiavellian instincts in people who achieve financial success.

George Soros is a brilliant strategist and trader and at the same time a generous philanthropist. He is a unique and admirable person who set out to undermine totalitarian regimes behind the Iron Curtain, to bring democracy and an open society to Eastern Europe. He is not a zealous advocate of laissez faire economics because, first, he does not believe markets are efficient and, second, as he puts it,

> I don't believe competition leads to the best allocation of resources. I
> don't consider the survival of the fittest the most desirable outcome. I
> believe we must strive for certain fundamental values, such as social
> justice, which cannot be attained by unrestrained competition (Soros,
> 1995).

Market economy and fierce competition provide survival for the fittest, but survival for the fittest is the law of the jungle, or the law of the ocean, where the big nullifies the small. In the ocean, the shark is an efficient animal, but the concepts of mercy, solidarity and compassion do not exist in its world. What is good for the bottom of the ocean is not good for a society of human beings. Alas, tragically, we introduced the law of the jungle into our daily lives. And it is a great misfortune that these days the US is the only superpower, because, for all practical purposes, it is the US which pushes the rest of the world towards a valueless way of life. The US has always been a country of no social justice, where loyalty is to the dollar and where, contrary to common belief, democracy is diminishing.

Sweden, for example, is a Western democracy in which egalitarianism has been the bedrock concept of culture. It is a pity that Sweden finds itself in a position whereby the government has to slim down its welfare state because of its difficulty in competing in 'the fittest survives' environment. Likewise, Canada's Prime Minister, Jean Chrétien, during a speech in March 1998 at the Economic Club of New York, was right to point out that "there will always be people who are not able to manage on their own, and it is the role of government to help them" (*The Globe and Mail*, March 4, 1998). Similarly, Britain's prime minister, Tony Blair, stands out as a remarkable leader. He fully understands that providing opportunities for entrepreneurs is necessary and important, but at the same time he acknowledges that the government has to provide for those who are not taken care of by market forces.

In his illuminating book, *Something's Wrong Somewhere*, Christopher Lind describes the decline of Canadian farmers in Saskatchewan and the effect of globalization in general.

> Under this revolutionary change and influence, community was reduced to a set of commercial transactions. Under the new imperative of the market, communities were ripped up, transplanted and destroyed on a regular basis… The net effect of this isolation and elevation of competitiveness as the dominant moral norm is to subordinate questions of social justice to questions of economic efficiency" (Lind, 1995).

The belief that pursuing self-interest serves the common good is a myth. If we do not replace market economy and indifference by moral economy and compassion, social collapse will ensue. Rabbi Shlomo Carlebach, one of the great Jewish educators of this century, was fully aware of the consequences of such behaviour. He said that "the world was balanced on our activity to help one another. Should someone fail to assist another person, the world could be destroyed" (Cooper, 1997).

Interestingly, there is a matrix which raises the possibility that the US will be destroyed. The minimal appearance of the expression *the US will be destroyed*, תשמד ארהב, in skip -204, coincides with the minimal skip, -6, of the year *765*, תשסה, (September 2004 to September 2005). One line above the encoded year *765* is written the word *in the year*, בשנה. In very close proximity is written the name *Bush*, coinciding with the words *pronounced my name*. This matrix is congruent with the time window for Judgment Day as indicated in the first chapter. The coming holocaust, I believe, will be the last punitive action to be implemented by God. Kabbalah teaches us that thereafter, a millennium of peace and harmony will ensue.

```
רתקראואתמממקראיקדשלהקריבאשהליהוהעלהומנחההזב
שמיניושבתונולקחתמלכמב(ה)ומהראשונפריעצהדרכרכפתת
ותהוושבתיאתבניישראלבמ(ה)וציאיאותממארצמצרימאני
למלדרתיכמעלהמנרההטהה(ר)יערכאתהנרותלפנייהוהת
ניריהוהתמידמאתהבנייש(א)לברךתעולמולמיתהלאהרנול
מאמןושלמיתבתדבריילמטה(ד)נויניחהובמשמרלפרשלהמע
דהכגרכאזרחבנקלמי(ה)מ(ש)(ש)מיוהואישכייכהכלנפשאדממות
אנייהוהאלהיכמיודברמ(ש)האלבנייישראלויוציאואתה
תזמרכרמכואספתואתתבו(א)ת(ה)ו(ב)(ש)נ(ה)השביעתהשבתשבתוני
תהיהכלתבואתה(ה)לאכל(ו)(ס)פרתלכ(ש)בעתלמ(ת)שני משבעעשני
מאישאלאחדזתויראישאלמשפחתותשבוירבלהוראשנתהחמש
```

○ *the US will be destroyed*   ⬠ *in the year*   ☐ *765 (2005)*
__ *pronounced my name*   ○ *Bush*

Somehow, somewhere, humanity took a wrong turn. Governments created systems which encourage selfishness and greed. In society we implemented the law of the jungle according to which the fittest survives. No wonder that in such an atmosphere people exhibit an infinite desire to receive and almost a zero desire to share. The milieu of materialism, selfishness and greed brought economic affluence, but at the same time it also brought spiritual poverty and lack of social justice. One need not be a genius to understand that God does not appreciate a society which is materialistically affluent and spiritually bankrupt. In the same way that ancient societies worshiped the sun or the moon, or one icon or another, today's society worships money. Worshiping a matter or an image instead of worshiping God has not changed, only the medium is different. Unfortunately, people believe that making a fortune is heroic, whereas a true hero is a person who dispenses happiness.

In the first chapter, I wrote that God awarded us a first grace period which ends on March 29, 2001. As well, according to a few matrices, Judgment Day may take place in the years 2005/2006, which means that we may be granted another grace period. If God gave us a grace period, it is possible that there is a way to prevent the holocaust from happening. If such an option exists, it must be that the Absolute Good is still awaiting the Jewish people to abide by the covenant.

In my opinion, if there is a way to change the course of events, it lies with the people of Israel. I once mused on the possibility of people and corporations giving charity on a macroeconomic scale. In Israel, about sixteen percent of the population live below the poverty line. Just imagine how charity given on a macroeconomic scale would change the country. If Israelis were to embark on a campaign titled "Not a single person lives in Israel below the poverty line," the country would transform dramatically. Such a campaign will have implications far beyond solving the problem of poverty. It will also alleviate hostilities between secular and orthodox, as well as between Ashkenazi and Sepharadic Jews. Charity on a macroeconomic scale will activate a miracle, and Israel will be recognized as heaven on Earth. Under such circumstances, millions of Jewish people will immigrate to Israel, and eventually, the country will become what God intended it to be, light to the nations, אור לגויים. Probably, other countries will follow suit and in due course, a peaceful planet will be ready to enter the seventh millennium.

As naïve and as Utopian this idea sounds, it may very well be one recipe for preventing the holocaust from happening. Being charitable will certainly bring God happiness and make Him proud of His creation. This, however, will not suffice, for God did not encode the Torah for a few researchers to have a hobby. The Code must provide a proof that God exists, that He is all powerful and that He authored the Torah.

Chapter 3
Synopsis of Eliyahu's Death

Emotionally, the setting of Eliyahu Yaffe's death was very difficult for me to deal with. Evidently, this setting was encoded explicitly for me to decipher. This setting contains a specific instruction for me to bring justice, regardless of who is involved in the setting. The following verse appears in crucial matrices: *Dan shall judge his people as one of the tribes of Israel.* My family name is encoded in the continuation of this phrase, in skip 112. A few months went by before I was able to bring myself to do it. I tried to find reasons why I should not go ahead, but my life turned into a nightmare as time went by. I understood that this setting represented, among other things, a test God had chosen for me. Furthermore, I understood that if God encoded this setting in such detail, it must be that proving this setting in a court of law must constitute one of the conditions for redemption to take place.

While working on this setting I understood why I had to leave Israel after my father passed away in 1975. Furthermore, I understood the reasons behind many of my life experiences. During the time I deciphered the setting of Eliyahu's death, I received 'messages' in real life as well as via dreams. I cannot even start writing about the numerous unexplained events which came my way in real life. Profound mystical experiences followed which changed the course of my life.

In Israel, bus transportation is run by a national public company called Egged. Since the sixties, Egged has been purchasing thousands of Mercedes-Benz buses. For years, the fraud department of the police suspected that Egged executives accepted bribes to facilitate those bus purchases. A police investigation ensued, and the Israeli government initiated court proceedings in Germany to force Daimler-Benz to provide financial records of Egged deals. In 1997 the Israeli government won the lawsuit, and the German court ordered Daimler-Benz to comply with Israeli government demands.

A few years ago, one of Egged's top executives, by the name of Eliyahu Yaffe, decided to cooperate with the police and became their state witness. The police investigation intensified, but on Sunday, February 22, 1998, Eliyahu Yaffe died in Jesselson Heart Centre in Shaarei Zedek Medical Centre in Jerusalem. Three years before he died, he had had a heart by-pass operation, but thereafter he had carried on a normal life. On February 20, 1998, Eliyahu Yaffe had checked into the hospital after having a fever for a few days. His situation deteriorated rapidly, and an angiocardiography was performed; the next day he died. The hospitalization report describes a man who died because of his recent heart problem. Alas, the Torah Code raises the possibility that Eliyahu Yaffe was murdered. The information about Eliyahu's death does not emanate from one isolated matrix but from numerous matrices which interweave and point to the same conclusion. God encoded this setting in a decisive and exquisite manner. As I understood my role in this setting and the explicit instruction to bring justice, I wrote in 1998 a general description of this setting to Israel's Attorney General, Elyakim Rubinstein. Alas, Daphna Barnai from the Office of the Attorney General wrote to me that the type of evidence I have, referring to the Torah Code, cannot be admitted by a court of law. Yet, she adds, "It must be stressed, that the above is by no means a statement of opinion or recommendation by the Attorney General as to the specific content of this matter." I later wrote to State Attorney Edna Arbel but received a similar answer.

On August 2, 1999, an article titled "Mercedes allegedly paid Egged heads millions of dollars in bribes" was published in *The Jerusalem Post* by Heidi Gleit. She writes that "The Israel Police yesterday alleged in the Tel Aviv Magistrate's Court that Mercedes paid former Egged chairman Shlomo Levin millions of dollars so that the bus company would buy Mercedes buses throughout the '80s and early '90s. The Israel Police, with the help of the German police and the FBI, has been investigating the case for the past three years." Another article on the same subject was published in the Israeli newspaper *Yediot Ahronot* on August 5, 1999.

The term *Eliyahu's murder*, רצח אליהו, is encoded only once in the Torah in skip -3362. The word *murder* in text, in skip -1, crosses the word *murder* in the encoded *Eliyahu's murder*. In very close proximity is encoded in the same skip the name *Yaffe* and crossing it in text the word *the family*. One crucial detail emerges from this matrix; a line which crosses the name *Eliyahu* in the word *Eliyahu's murder* reads *the man whose eye is open*, הגבר שתם העין. Rashi interprets this line, saying that the eye socket is open, *that his eye is missing… who is blind in one eye.* Another interpretation of this line by *Eekar Siftei Chachamim* states that *he had good vision only in one eye.* The phrase *the man whose eye is open* appears only twice in the Torah, both times in the Book of Numbers, in chapter 24. Indeed, Eliyahu Yaffe had had an eye surgery and had poor vision in one eye. An Israeli private detective confirmed that Eliyahu Yaffe did not have good vision in one eye. Later, I received a similar confirmation during a telephone conversation I had with Eliyahu's wife, Mrs. Yonna Yaffe. An instruction to disseminate this information appears in a line which crosses the word *Eliyahu's murder*: *your sins were proclaimed*. Barry Roffman, a retired military war-plan writer and an avid Bible Code investigator, calculated the probability for this matrix to be one in 232 billion (2.32225E+11), provided the findings were thought of a priori (see appendix).

- ○ *Eliyahu's murder*
- ⎿⎾ *murder*
- ⬠ *Yaffe*
- ___ *the family*
- ⎾‾⎤ *your sins were proclaimed*
- ▭ *he had good vision only in one eye*

```
מנתנאתישראלעברבגבלוריטישראלמעליוויסעו
בבקרויחבשואתאתנ①ילכעמשרימואבויחראפאלה
מבלעמבנובערונאמה⬠א⬠גברשתמהעי⟨ין⟩נאמשמעאמריא
מאלפוארבעעמאותבנ⟨ר⟩כפתלימשⓟⓒⓗתמליהצאלמשפ
שנהומונחתמסלתבל⟨ל⟩הבשמנשלש⟨ⓗⓣ⟩עשרנימלפרהאח
מואתכלחילמבזדזו⟨ר⟩ⓐⓣⓗכלעריהמבמושבתמואתכלט
החטאתמליה⟨ה⟩ⓗⓓעⓗⓣⓐאתכמ⟨כמ⟩אשרתמצאאתכמכבנולכ
מלכמלגבולקדמהמⓒⓗ⟨ⓒ⟩עינשפמהוירדהגבלמשפמ
ואלההדבריאמאשרד⟨ב⟩משהאלכלישראלבעברהירדנ
ורואנשיהמלחמהחמהמקרבהמחנהכאשרנשבעיהוהלהמ
ינתכמלעיניהעמימאשריⓣשמעונאתכלהחקימהאלה
```

The expression *Yaffe's murder*, רצח יפה, in its minimal skip 369 is also a very significant one. Next to *Yaffe's murder* is encoded in the same skip the word *Jerusalem*, the city in which he lived and died. Eliyahu Yaffe was a state witness and indeed, next to *Yaffe's murder* is written in plain text *the death of the witness*. Also in plain text, the word *the family* is crossing the family name *Yaffe*. The probability of this matrix was calculated by Barry Roffman and was found to be one in 1,522,071,021 (see appendix).

תנמושבכושימבסלעקנככיאמיהיהלבערקין
עורוהנהאישמבנייישראלבאויקרבאלאחירא
והיתהלוולזרעואחריוברירתכהנתעולמתחת
מעלהלביתאבתמכלא⟨צ⟩אב⟨י⟩ישראלוידברמש
יהותבלעאתמואתק⟨ה⟩⟨ח⟩מותהעד⟨ב⟩הבאכלהאשאת
ראוננבארצכנענ⟨ה⟩⟨י⟩הירבנייהודהלמשפחת
שמאותבניוסספלמ⟨ש⟩פחתממנשהואפרימבנים
ערנמשפחתהערנ⟨ר⟩אל⟨ה⟩המשפחתבניאפרימלפקד
שפחתהימנהלישורי⟨מ⟩שפחתהישוילבריעהמשפ
עיטנחלתואישלפיפקדיריתנחלתואכבגור
פנייהוהויהירופקדיהמשלשהועשרימאלפכל

○ *Yaffe's murder*
▭ *the death of the witness*
○ *Jerusalem*
__ *the family*

In a matrix generated by the name *Eliyahu Yaffe*, אליהו יפה, in skip 3470 we can see the phrase *the man whose eye is open* written just beside his name. The same line, containing the phrase *the man whose eye is open*, also contains the term *in the End of Days*. This is not the minimal appearance of the name *Eliyahu Yaffe* in the Torah, but it is significant, for the word משפחת, *the family*, crosses Eliyahu's family name.

למרימצאושלשתכמאלאהלאמלמועדוייצאושלשתמויירדיהוהבעמודענניריע
עתיאמראלהמחי⟨א⟩ינאמיהוהאמלאכאשרדברתמבאזניכנאעשהלכמבמד
לעדתכהנעדימעל⟨י⟩הוהואהרנמההוהואכיתלונועלירוושלחמשהלקראלד
נמלכלתנופתב⟨ו⟩ישראלכלכנתתימולבנינכולבנתיכאתכלחקנעולמכלטה
קצהגבולכנענבר⟨ה⟩נאבארצכלכלאנענערבשדהובכרמולאנשנתהמיבארדרכהם
וגדולהועתהתשב⟨ו⟩נאבזהגמאתמהלילהואדעהמהיספיהוהדרבערעמיויבא
באחריתהימים⟨ן⟩⟨ו⟩שאמשלווייאמרנאמרנאמבלעמבנובערונאמ⟨ה⟩הגברשתמהעי⟨ן⟩
חתהשלמיאלהמש⟨פ⟩חתנפתלילמשפחתמופקדימשפחתמוארבעימאלפוארב
אתעשורומתרדע⟨ה⟩היהלכמועשיתמעלהלריחניחזחליהוהפרבנבקראחד
ההיולבנייישראלבדברבלעמלמסרמעליהוהעלדברפעורותהיהמגפהב

○ *Eliyahu Yaffe*   __ *the family*
▭ *he had good vision only in one eye*   ⌐ *in the end of days*

The equivalent date of Eliyahu's death in the Hebrew calendar is 26, כו, of the month of *Shvat,* שבט. The following matrix generated by this date, כו שבט, contains a revealing phrase: *Eliyahu… who will die very suddenly.* Above the name *Eliyahu* is encoded his family name, *Yaffe,* together with the word *of the family.* Some of these matrices contain more information, and there are more matrices describing this setting. For obvious reasons this material cannot be published at this time.

```
שהגמליאלבבנפדהצורוצבאורופקדיהמשניימושלשימאלפומאתימומטה
בניישראלויפקדמשהכאשרצוהיהוהאתואתכלבבכורבבניישראלויהי
הלמועדוריהיופקדיהמלמשפחתמלביתאבתמאלפימושממאותושלשימא
זרוקדשהאליההוכייימותמתעליובפתעעפתאמוטמאראשנזרורונלחר
הכבשימבנוישנהחמשהזהקרבנאליצורבנשדיאורבנועמהחמישינשיאל
תאליובהעלתכאתהנרתאלמולפניהמנורהיאירושעתהנרותוישעשכן
דשאורימהבהארייכהענננעלהמשכנלשכנעלוויחנובניישראלולאיסע
ואצלתימנהרוחאשרעליכושמתיעלישאואשביומדלתמשאהעמולאתשאא
ריהארצוהיהמימימיבכרורייענביימיעלוויתרואתהארצמדברצנעדר
רתמאתהארצאראבעימיומימולשנהיומלשנהתשאותעונתיכמארבעימ
```

○ *26 Shvat (February 22)*   ▭ *Eliyahu*   ◇ *Yaffe*

⌐ *of the family*   __ *who will die very suddenly*

It is normal for people who love God and feel His presence to expect miracles to happen. In the book *Mesilat Yesharim* (*Path of the Just*), Ramchal was wondering why God had not provided him with the ability to perform miracles. Likewise, I was not surprised to read the following comment in one of the e-mails I received from professor Eliyahu Rips: "I think that only when the time of open miracles will return (and I do believe that we not very far from it), the code will gain acceptance and recognition."

The fraud department of the police in Israel has been investigating the Egged buses bribe case for years, but no one has been put on trial as of yet. Although the aggregate probability of all these matrices is one in billions, it is regrettable that the Israeli authorities do not take the Torah Code seriously. If the matrices that I have discovered describe a true event, and if evidence sufficient to establish this event as true can be found, this discovery would surely constitute a miracle.

Chapter 4
The Appearance of Kabbalah Topics in the Bible Code

Kabbalah aspires to explain the Divinity, the function of God in our lives. Kabbalah studies the relationship between Creator and created, between the Source of the light to the recipient of the light. Kabbalah is a knowledge base of Jewish mysticism and is divided into three fields: the study of Kabbalah for the purpose of acquiring knowledge, Kabbalistic meditation and practical Kabbalah. As for practising Kabbalah in real life, to the best of my knowledge, ancient rituals are not effective and have not been effective for a very long time. One of Kabbalah's cornerstones is the interaction between the world of souls and our physical world. As the level of spirituality on planet Earth has been continuously declining during the last 250 years, the world of souls has been reluctant to cooperate. This is not to say that there is no interaction these days with the world of souls, just that its scope is different and much more selective. Kabbalah deals with all aspects of life, with creation, with the Hebrew alphabet, with the world of souls and its interaction with our physical world, with reincarnation, with astrology and with the Age of Aquarius. The segment of practical Kabbalah which has always been effective is the one that has to do with the Hebrew alphabet. Ramak, the great Kabbalist, wrote that information was encoded in the Torah in skipping letters. Evidently, the Torah Code is an integral part of Kabbalah, and the Book of *Zohar* (Book of Splendor) deals with the alphabetical list and with the energy which corresponds to each letter. According to Kabbalah, God created the universe with the Hebrew alphabet.

The following matrix demonstrates that God gave us the Hebrew alphabet. The word *alphabet*, אלף בית, in its minimal skip in the Torah, 186, is encoded at the very beginning of the Book of Genesis. The verse which coincides with the word *alphabet* reads: *And God said, Behold I have given you.* In close proximity are encoded the two names of languages using the Hebrew alphabet: *Aramaic* and *Hebrew*.

בראשיתברראאלהים
ויקראאלהימלאורי ומולחשכקראלי להוי היערבוי הבקרי ומאחדוי א
היבקרי ומשני ויאמראלהימיקוו והמיממתחתהשמי מאלמקומאחדותראה
הארצדשאעשבעשבמזריעזרעלמי נהוועצעשהפרי אשרזרעובולמי נהווי רא
להארצוי היכני ועשאלהי מאתשני המארתהגזל מאתהמאורהגדללממשל
קרי ומרביעי ויאמראלהי מישרצוהמי שרצנפשחי הועוחיהועופי עופפעלהאר
תהמי מביומי מהעופי רבבארצי היערבוי הבקרי ומחמישי וי אמראלה
בצלמנוכדמותנוי רדובדגתהי מובעופהשמי מובבהמהובכלהארצובכ
מובכלחי ההרמשתעלהארצ ויאמראלהי מהנהנתתי לכמאתכלעשבזרעזרע
רעשוהוהנהטובומאדוי היערבוי היבקרי ומהששי ויכלוהשמי מוהארצוכ
ותהשמי מוהארצבהבראמברי ומעשותי הואלהי מארצושמי מוכלשי חהשד

○ alphabet
□ Aramaic
◇ Hebrew
▭ and God said, behold I have given you

Only a few people realize the power which is attributed to letters and therefore, to their given names. A combination of letters which form a name attracts various energies from the spiritual world. The significance of given names can be seen in the following matrix, which is generated by the minimal and actually, the only appearance of the word *spiritual world*, עולם רוחני, in the Torah, in skip 170. The five lines which cross the words *spiritual world* articulate the subject of a given name to a newborn. The five lines read as follows: *and bore a son, and she called his name... I have bore him three sons: therefore was his name called... therefore called his name... and called his name... and called her name...*

The issue of a given name is so important that at times, when a person suffers misfortune and illnesses, a Kabbalist will recommend to change the person's name. The new name brings different energies which will change the essence of his being and therefore, may alter the course of his life.

ראתהלכמתתיאתהלאישאחרשבהעמדיריעבדיעקבברחלשבעשנימויהיוב
באאתהאליוויבאאליהויתנתנלבלבנלהאתזלפהשפחתוללאהבתוושפחהוהיהב
גמאתזאתהבעבדהאשרתעבדעמדיעודשבסנימאחרותיעשיעקבכנריימלא
ישנראהלאהויפתחאתרחמהורחלעקרהתהרלאהותלדבנותקראשמוראוב
עתההפעמילוהאישיאליכילדתילושהבניימעלכנקראשמולויותהרע
וריחראפיעקבברחלויאמרהתחתאלהיםאנכיאשרמנעממכפריבטנותאמר
בקלירויתנליבנעלכנקראהשמשמרהנדנותהרעודיתלדבלההשפחתרחלבנשניל
הליעקבובנותאמרלאהבהגדרתקראאתשמהוגדותלדזלפהשפחתלאהבנשנילי
יבנכיותאמרלהמעטהמטקנחתכאתאישילקחתנשיולקחתגמאתדודאיבניותאמררחללכן
ותהרותלדליעקבבנחמישיותאמרלאהנתנאלהיםשכרישארנתתישפחתיל
ילדהבתוותקראאתשמהאשרויהוזכראלהרמאתרחלויישמעאליהאלהימורפת
קומיולארצתנהאתנהאנשיואתילדיאשרעבדתיאתכבהבהנואלכהכיאתהידעת
אשרהיהמקנכאתיכימעטאשרהיהלכלפניוירצפרצלרבויברכיהוהאתכלרגל

○ spiritual world
▭ and bore a son, and she called his name
___ I have bore him three sons: therefore was his name called
⌐ ̄ therefore called his name
⌊___⌋ and called his name
○ and called her name

Once we discuss the importance of names, let us see how the topic of God's seventy-two names is encoded in the Torah. The Book of *Zohar* tells us that God has seventy-two names. These names originate from three verses, each containing seventy-two letters from the Book of Exodus 14:19-21. The first verse reads *Then the angel of God who went before the host of Israel, moved and went behind them; and the pillar of cloud moved from before them and stood behind them.* The second verse continues *coming between the host of Egypt and the host of Israel; and there was the cloud and the darkness; and the night passed without one coming near the other all night.* And the third verse reads *Then Moses stretched out his hand over the sea; and the Lord drove the sea back by a strong east wind all night, and made the sea dry land, and the waters were divided.* To construct the first name, we take the first letter of the first verse, then the last letter of the second verse, and then the first letter of the third verse. In a similar manner, we can construct the second name: the second letter of the first verse, the second letter from the end of the second verse, and the second letter of the last verse. Each of the seventy-two names contains three letters.

In the following matrix, you can see the encoded phrase *the names of God*, שמות האל. Next to this word is written *two and seventy* (72). Four lines below we can read *And she called the name of the Lord*.

○ *the names of God*   ▭ *two and seventy (72)*   ⌐⌐ *and she called the name of the Lord*

The term *The Creator of everything*, בורא הכל, in skip 728 is encoded at the very beginning of Genesis. It coincides with the verse *In the beginning God created the heavens and the earth*. Other relevant phrases read *And God said, Behold, I have given you* as well as *The Lord God had made*.

○ *The Creator of everything*
▭ *In the beginning God created the heavens and the earth*
⌐ *and God said, Behold, I have given you*
⌐⌐ *the Lord God had made*

The Torah Code illustrates the importance of Kabbalah and the Book of *Zohar*. A matrix generated by the word *Kabbalah*, קבלה, in skip 22 from the Book of Leviticus shows the word *Zohar* in skip 20 and in tight configuration are written twice *it is most holy*, crossing each of these two words.

```
בגדאשריזהעליהתכבבסבמקום
קדשוכליחרשאשרתבשלבוישב
רואמבבכלינחשתבשלהוומרקוש
טפבמימכלזכרבבכהנימיאכלא
תהקדשקדשימןהואוכלחטאתאש
ריובאמדמהאלאהלמועדלכפר
בקדשלאתאכלבאשתשרפותאתת
ורתהאשמקדשימהרואבמקו
מאשרישחטואתהעלהיהישחטואת
האשמואתדמויזרקעלהמזבחס
ביבואתכלחלבויקרימבמננוא
תהאליהואתהחלבהמכסהאתהק
רבואתשתיהכליתואתהחלבאש
עליהנאשרעלהכסלימואתהי
תרתעלהכבדעלהכליתיסירנה
והקטיראתמהכהננהמזבחהאשה
```

○ *Kabbalah*
□ *Zohar*
___ *it is most holy*

A few elements determine the course of a person's life; his deeds (his behaviour, his choices), his birth chart, the letters which comprise his given name, the long-term ledger page of his soul and the *Sfirah's* energy from which his soul originated. The ten *Sfirot* are spiritual filters that transform light and energy into distinct traits.

As we know, scientists claim that a person uses only five percent of his brain. For thousands of years people wondered what was in the other ninety-five percent. To the best of my understanding, the ninety-five percent of the capacity of a person's brain encompasses this "baggage"; his birth chart, the energies corresponding to the letters of his given name, his long-term ledger page of his soul and his *Sfirah's* energy from which his soul originated. We do not have access to information stored in this part of our brains, nor do we understand the interaction which takes place between the part we are conscious of and the part we are not conscious of. Yet, in this inaccessible ninety-five percent part of our brains dwell as well our misdeeds from past lives. In a mysterious way, we are brought to relive these experiences during this life, in the hope we will handle them better. In the same way, this unreachable ninety-five percent part enables communications from the world of souls to be recorded in our brains.

A person's birth chart is defined as a combination of tools, a certain potential and a unique soul vitality which were poured into him at the moment of his birth so he is able later to accomplish the needed rectification (*Tikun*, in Hebrew) of his soul.

The first element – human behaviour, the deeds committed in a man's life, making a choice – represent the most relevant factor as to the direction and the outcome of his life. As to the other elements, it will be a futile exercise to classify them in accordance to their importance. Their weight and their influence may vary in the course of a person's life. In other words, the dominance of each of these elements at a particular time and the balance between them is only known to God.

Concerning a person's birth chart, there is a general misconception as to what astrology is all about. Contrary to common belief, astrology is not a predicting device. Nor can it provide the answers to questions you are asking. Apart from symbolizing a combination of tools, a certain potential and a unique soul vitality, a birth chart serves as a conduit for energies transmitted via planets. Furthermore, a birth chart is a tool for a soul, not for a person. As one uses a watch or a calendar to tell time, a soul uses a birth chart as a reference to time. What we call "past lives" is just different time windows in the life of a soul. As a life of a soul is a very long one and as previous birth charts of the people in whom the soul lived are relevant, the soul uses astronomy as a reference to time. Similarly, the concepts "past" and "future" exist for us, but not for God nor for the world of souls. For God, there is a blueprint of creation, the roots, from which branches grow. During our lifetime, we occupy a certain horizontal area of the branches, represented by the length of our life expectancy. The boundaries – what preceded our birth and what will follow after we die – exist for us, but not for the blueprint. Just think about it: in one hundred years from now no one whom you know, not relatives nor friends, will be alive. There will be a different set of human beings who will inhabit our planet, or in other words, who will occupy another section of the blueprint.

The first reason why practical astrology fails miserably is that the birth charts of the people where your soul had lived in the past are relevant, and an astrologer has no way of knowing them. Second, as the weight of the different elements fluctuate continuously, an astrologer does not know when a chart is more active and when it is less active. Astrologers invented all kind of "readings" and "progressions" because they do not understand why sometimes a birth chart "works" and at other times a birth chart "does not work."

Kabbalah deals with astrology. Judaism has never denied that astrology is valid and effective. Jewish sages like Rabbi Seadia Gaon (882-942), Iben-Gabirol (Rashbag, 1020-1057), Yitzhak Abrabanel (1437-1508) and Rabbi Moshe Chayim Luzzatto (Ramchal, 1707-1747) gave astrology great importance. The Book of *Zohar* and the *Book of Creation* deal extensively with astrology, for the planets constitute an integral part of the laws of nature which God established. Rabbi Luzzatto (Ramchal) writes that the planets serve as vessels which transmit God's plan from the spiritual world to the physical one. Hence, forces of existence and chronological events which dwell in the roots, in the world of souls, are being pulled down to the branches, to our physical world, via the planets.

Ecclesiastes writes in chapter 3:1 that *For every thing there is a season; and a time for every matter under heaven.* Evidently, the structure of the solar system implies that every event is unique and unrepeatable. Hence, it behooves that each time a person misses an opportunity, this exact opportunity associated with its particular energy is lost forever. Think for a minute about a couple having a candlelight evening at a rustic restaurant. The food is terrific, the atmosphere is romantic and there is magic in the air. They fall in love with the place and a month later they dine again at the same restaurant, wishing to recreate the experience. Even though everything seems to be the same, they find the atmosphere to be a bit different and the magic not quite there. It is not quite there because every event contains a delicate balance of numerous variables which make it unique. Repetitions are positive and pleasant but for one reason or another, the exactness is unrepeatable.

The minimal appearance in the Torah of the words *birth chart*, מפת לידה, in skip 451, coincides with the expression *predetermined*, as well as with the words *at your times*. The old Hebrew word for *astronomy*, תכונה, is encoded in skip 12, and in the same line is encoded the word *destiny* in skip -5.

```
לאזרחהארצובירומהקימאתהמשכנכסההענגנאתהמשכנלאהלהעדתובערבי
נעליויריחנורבנישראלולאיסעורבהעלתורסעועלפייהוהיחנורועלפיי
נייהוהאלהיכמורושעתהממאריכמוביומשמחתכמ(ה)חו(ה)במועדיכמורבראשיח
עוגשלמיאלבנצורישדירועלצבאמטהבניגדאליס(פ)נדעואלונסעורהקהת
למולדתיאלכויראמראלנאתהעזנבאתנוכירעלכנידע(ת)חנתנורבמדברוהייתל
ותה(ת)אוהוישבוויב(כ)וגמבנישראל(ה)יאמרומייאס(מ)ל(ו)בש(ר)זכרנ(ו)את(ה)ד(ג)ה
ישאהאמנאתהירנקעלהאדמהאשרנשבעתהתלאבתיומא(נ)ליבשרלתתלכלהעמה
ולאחזמשהימימולאעשרהימימולאעשרימימ(ד)חם(שם)ימימעדאשרוצאמאפ
נהשמהאחדדאלדדושמהשנימידדותנחעולהמהרוח(ה)מ(ה)הבכתבימ(ו)לאיצאוה
בעמויריכיהובעממכהרבההמאדוירקראאתהשמהמקומההואקברותהתאוהכיש
מנתיהוהביטומדועלאירואעבדיומשהדברבעבדימבמשהויחראפיויחראפיהוהבמוילכו
```

○ *birth chart*   ▭ *predetermined*   ⌐ *at your times*
□ *astronomy*   ○ *destiny*

The prohibition of practising astrology does not emanate from astrology's being null and void. Rather, the classical explanation is that this forbiddance originates from the fear that people would mistakenly believe that their destiny is predetermined and unchangeable. For all practical purposes, one should not delve into astrology, first, because astrology is a tool for souls, not for the individual. Second, the birth charts of people a soul served in the past are relevant, and an astrologer has no access to this information. Third, an astrologer has no way of knowing the weight of a birth chart versus the weight of other elements of a person's being at a given time. Fourth, to a certain extent, a person can change his astrological sign or a component of his sign with the combination of his deeds and his prayers. Fifth, during particular times and for special reasons, God may overrule the astrological influence during the course of a person's life.

The Torah Code validates the existence of the world of souls. The term *world of souls*, עולם נשמות, is encoded in the Torah only once, in skip 11420. One line above is written *tombstone on grave*. Coinciding with *world of souls* is encoded the words *the souls* in skip -5. In the text, one line below *world of souls* is written *after death* as well as *and they died*. The abbreviation in Hebrew of the term *the next world* is encoded in skip -13. This matrix proves that the world of souls exists, and that it has to do with what comes after life.

```
ו י ד ב ר א ל ע פ ר ו נ ב א ז נ י ע מ ה א ר צ ל א מ ר א כ א מ א ת ה ל ו ש מ ע נ י נ ת ת י כ ס פ ה ש ד ה ק
א ת צ א נ ל ב נ א ח י א מ ו ר י ש ק י ע ק ב ל ר ח ל ו י ש א א ת ק ל ו ר י ב כ ו ר י ג ד י ע ק ב ל ר ח ל כ י
ר ח ל ו ת ק ב ר ב ד ר כ א פ ר ת ה ה ו א ב י ת ל ח מ ו י צ ב י ע ק ב מ צ ב ה ע ל ק ב ר ת ה ה ו א מ צ ב ת ק
י ש ר א ל ש ב ע י ב ן ו כ ה ב א י מ כ י ה ה ר ע ב ב א ר צ כ נ ע נ ו ס פ ה ו א ה ש ל י ט ע ל ה א
י מ י נ י ש ר א ל ו ר י ש א ל י ו ר י ש ל ח י ש ר א ל א ת י מ י נ ו י ש ת ע ל א ר א ש א פ ר י מ ו ה ו א ה
ת ה ק ר ח י ו א ל ע ז ר ב נ א ה ר נ ל ק ה ל ו מ ב נ ו ת פ ו ט י א ל ל א ש ה ו ת ל ד ל ו א ת פ י נ ח ס
כ ו ר א ת מ ד ב ב נ י כ ת פ ד ה ה י ה כ י י ש א ל כ ב ב נ כ מ ח ר ל א מ ר מ ה ז א ת ו א מ ר ת א ל י ו ב ח ז
י ר כ ה א י ש א ת ע ב ד ו ר א ו א ת א מ ת ו ב ש ב ט ו מ ת ת ח ת י ד ו נ ק מ י נ ק ם א כ א מ י ו מ א ו ר ו מ
ה ו ה ו ש ב צ ת ה כ ת נ ת ש ש י ת ע ש י ת מ צ נ פ ת ש ש ו א ב נ ט ת ע ש ה מ ע ש ה ר ק מ ו ל ב נ י א ה ר נ ת
ס כ ש ע ר ה צ ר א ת י ת ד ת ה מ ש כ נ ו א ת י ת ד ת ה ח צ ר ו א ת מ י ת ר י ה מ א ת ב ג ד י ה ש ר ד ל ש
ר י ב ו א ת מ ל י ה ו ה ו א ל ה מ ז ב ח ל א י ע ל ו ל ר י ח נ י ח ז ל כ ל ק ר ב נ ו מ נ ח ת כ ב מ ל ח ת מ ל
כ ל ב י ת י ש ר א ל י ב כ ו א ת ה ש ר פ ה א ש ר ש ר פ י ה ו ה ו מ פ ת ח א ה ל מ ו ע ד ל א ת צ א ו פ נ ת מ
ל מ ש ה א ח ר י מ ו ת ש נ י ב נ י א ה ר נ ב ק ר ב ת מ ל פ נ י י ה ו ה ו י מ ת ו ר י א מ ר י ה ו ה א ל מ ש
מ ו י ד ב ר י ה ו ה א ל מ ש ה ל א מ ר ד ב ר א ל ב נ י י ש ר א ל א ל א מ ר ב ח ד ש ה ש ב י ע י ב א ח ד ל ח ד
ע ש ו י ד ב ר י ה ו ה א ל מ ש ה ו א ל א ה ר נ ל א מ ר א י ש ע ל ד ג ל ו ב א ת ל ב י ת א ב ת מ י ח נ ו
```

○ world of souls
□ the souls
⌐⌐ tombstone on grave
▭ after death
⌐⌐ and they died
△ abbreviation of 'the next world'

The Torah Code elucidates on the phenomenon of reincarnation, as demonstrated in the following matrix. The meeting between the encoded words *reincarnation*, גלגול, in skip 500 and *souls*, נשמות, in skip -1 coincides with the following phrase: *at the beginning we are brought to reincarnate* (my translation). In close proximity are encoded the words *the sign of the zodiac, soul, spirit*.

```
מ ו י י ר א ו ו י א מ ר א ל ה מ י ע ק ב ב א ב י ה מ א ת י מ ש כ ל ת מ י ו ס פ א י נ נ ו ו ש מ ע ו נ נ א י נ נ
כ ל ו ל א כ ל א ת ה ש ב ר א ש ר ה ב י א ו מ מ צ ר י מ ו י א מ ר א ל י ה מ א ב י ה מ ש ב ו ש ב ר ו ל נ ו
ש א ל ה א י ש ל נ ו ו ל מ ו ל ד ת נ ו ל א מ ר ה ע ו ד א ב י כ מ ח י ה י ש ל כ מ א ח ו נ ג ד ל ו ע ל פ י
ע מ י מ ו י א מ ר א ל ה מ י ש ר א ל א ב י ה מ א ת נ א פ ו א ז א ת ע ש ו ק ח ו מ ז מ ר ת ה א ר צ ב כ ל
י ש כ ל ת י ו י ק ח ו ה א נ ש י מ א ת ה מ נ ח ה ה ז א ת ו מ ש נ ה כ ס פ ל ק ח ו ב י ד מ ו א ת ב נ י מ ן
ב ב א מ ת ח ת י נ ו ב ת ח ל ה א נ ח נ ו מ ו ב א י מ ל ה ת ל ע ל י נ ו ל ה ת נ פ ל ע ל י נ ו ו ל ק
נ ו מ י ש מ כ ס פ נ ו ב א מ ת ח ת י נ ו ר ד י א מ ר ש ל ו מ ל כ מ א ל ת י ר א ו א ל ה י כ מ ו א ל ה י א ב
ח ו ר ל ו א ר צ ה ו י ש א ל ל ה מ ל ש ל ו מ ו י א מ ר ה ש ל ו מ א ב י כ מ ה ז ק נ א ש ר א מ ר ת מ ה ע ו
מ ו ל ח מ י ש י מ ו ל ו ל ב ד ו ו ל ה מ ל ב ד ו ל מ צ ר י מ ה א כ ל י מ א ת ו ל ב ד מ כ י ל א י ו כ
כ ל ו נ ש א ת ו ש י מ כ ס פ א י ש ב פ י א מ ת ח ת ו ו א ת ג ב י ע י ג ב י ע ה כ ס פ ת ש י מ ב פ י א מ ת
מ ו י ד ב ר א ל ה מ א ת ה ד ב ר י מ ה א ל ה ל ה ו י א מ ר ו א ל י ו ל מ ה י ד ב ר א ד נ י כ ד ב ר י מ ה א ל
א י ש א ת א מ ת ח ת ו א ר צ ה ו י פ ת ח ו א י ש א מ ת ח ת ו ר י ח פ ש ב ג ד ו ל ה ח ל ו ב ק ט נ כ כ ל ה ו
ה י מ מ צ א א ת ע נ ו ע ב ד י כ ה נ נ ו ל ע ב ד י מ ל א ד נ י ג מ א נ ח נ ו ג מ א ש ר נ מ צ א ה ג ב י ע ב
ל ד ז ק נ י מ ק ס ט נ ו א ח י ו מ ת ו י ו ת ר ה ו א ל ב ד ל א מ ו ו א ב י ו א ה ב ו ו ת א מ ר א ל ע ב ד
ח י נ ו ה ק ט נ א ת נ ו ו י ר ד נ ו כ י ל א נ ו כ ל ל ר א ו ת פ נ י ה א י ש ו א ח י נ ו ה ק ט נ א י נ נ ו
ו מ ת ו ה ו ר י ד ו ע ב ד י כ א ת ש י ב ת ע ב ד כ א ב י נ ו ב י ג ו נ ש א ל ה כ י ע ב ד כ ע ר ב א ת ה נ
```

○ *reincarnation*   ▭ *souls*   □ *spirit*
○ *soul*   △ *the sign of the zodiac*
⌐_⌐ *at the beginning we are brought to reincarnate*

     The next matrix deals with the issue of the various parts of the soul. This array is generated by the minimal appearance of the phrase *parts of soul*, חלקי נפש, in skip -4086. The Book of *Zohar* tells us that the soul consists of five parts. Nevertheless, in this matrix, the phrase which crosses the words *parts of soul* speaks about *first row*, *second row*, *third row* and *fourth row*. One line above the encoded words *parts of soul* is written in text the word *brain*. The word *the souls* is encoded in close proximity. The encoded words *parts of soul* coincide as well with the term *live flesh*. We can see that according to the Torah Code, the minimal appearance of the words *parts of souls* show that there are four parts to a person's soul. The Torah tells us that the part of our soul which is called *nefesh* is physically in the blood. This part is permanently in the body, for it keeps the body alive. The other two parts of the soul, *ruach* and *neshama*, enter the human body at a later stage, not at birth. Another part of the soul is permanently in heaven.

עתשנירששמשזרמעשהרקמעמדיהמארבעהואדניהמארבעהכלעלמודיהחצרסביבמחשקים
ואתשוקהתתרומהאשרהונפואשרהורהרמאילהמלאיממאשרלאהרנומאשרלבניורוהיהלאה
מצרימסרומהרמנהדרכאשרצויתמעשהולהמעגלמסכהויהמסכהויהורוליזבחולריריאמראול
תתעשהלכבכבוריקצירחסטיהמגהאסיפתקרפתההשנגלשלשפעמימבשנהיראהכלזכורכאתפ
ירשמנהקרשימואדניהמכספשהעשרהעשרהמכסנייאדנימשנייאדנימתתחתהקרשהאחדוריעש
הטורהאחדוהטורהשנינפכספריילהמהטורהשלישילשמשבוואחלמהוהטורהרביעי
מהאלמקומהדשנבוסעאתובבמפיולאיבדילוהקטירראתוהכהנהמזבחהעלהעצימאשרעל
אחתמאלהוהתודהאשרחטאעליוהביאאתאשמולייהוהעלחטאתואשרחטאהבהמנהצאנכ
משחתבניומאשיהיהוהביומחריבאתמלכהנכליהוהאשרצוהיהיהלהלתתלהמביוממשחתאת
החלוריביהטמאובינהטהורולהורתאתבנייישראלאתכלהחקימאשרדבריהוהאליהמביד
הנאתהבשרהשרהחיוטמאולטמאהורלההטמאהואצרעתהתהואוכיישובהבשרהחיונהפכללבנובא
רגלוהימניותעלמקומדמהאשאמוהנותרמנהשמנאשרעלכפהכהנירתנעלראשהמטהרלכפרע
דכלקהלישראלויצאאלהמזבחהאשרלפנייהוהוכפרעליוולקחמדמהפרומדמהשעירונת

○ parts of soul	☐ the souls	⬠ brain
▭ first row	▬ second row	⬟ third row
⌴ fourth row	⬡ live flesh	

During sleep, the parts of the soul which are called *ruach* and *neshama* leave the body and travel up to unite with the part that is permanently in heaven. Jewish sages labeled sleep as "the younger sister of death." In the Gemara, sleep is measured as "one sixtieth part of death." This is the reason why the very first prayer of gratitude to God said each morning is "I gratefully thank you, O living and eternal King, for You have returned my soul within me with compassion…." We thank the Lord for returning our souls to our bodies because when we were asleep, parts of our souls were not in our body.

For thousands of years people debated the subjects of destiny versus free choice. We have always wondered about the function of God in our lives. Continuously, people pray for His Light and for His Providence. We ask God to give to us from His Light because everything that comes from the Divine is in the form of Light, in the same way that everything that comes from Evil is in the form of veil. One of the pillars of religion is the obligation to pray three times a day. Prayers constitute repetitions, even exact repetitions. If you have had children, you know that toddlers love bed-time stories, and sometimes even ask to be told the same story over and over again. The same principle as a daily prayer works for these toddlers; repetitions, even exact repetitions, are good for us because repetitions constitute rituals. Rituals are good for us because in rituals we feel safe. We feel safe because we know what comes next. And what comes next for a God-fearing person is the knowledge that by following the Torah he becomes the embodiment of God's intention.

A person may be bright or foolish, tall or short, handsome or ugly, male or female, black or white in spite of his wishes. Think for a minute about your life on this planet as a horizontal line. At one point, regardless of your wishes, you were conceived in your mother's womb. Nine months thereafter, regardless of your wishes, you were born. Since the moment of your birth until this present day, against your wishes, you endured illnesses and maybe even misfortune. A day will come when, against your wishes, you will die. In other words, along the line of your life there seem to be inevitable stations. In between these stations you may exercise your choices. I wrote the word 'inevitable' but in fact, not all stations are inevitable. By exercising correct consecutive choices, you can move a station along the line. A person can move stations for better or for worse, depending on his deeds and misdeeds. In principal, some stations can be avoided, and others can be either mellowed or aggravated.

Eight hundred fifty two years ago Rabbi Moshe Ben-Mimon (*Rambam*) addressed the issue of God's beneficent care in his book *A Guide to the Confused*. The level of God's divine care available to a person is in direct relation to his love for God and his desire to be as close as possible to the Absolute Good. The non-believers are left with a general type of providence which applies to a group of people, rather than to an individual. Worse still, bad people and criminals reduce themselves to an animalistic level of beings and therefore, the providence which is available to them is thin and sparse, like the one which applies to cattle. The general rule is that the further one gets away from God, the more subject he is to randomness and chance.

The minimal skip of the word *providence*, השגחה, or *divine care*, 75, is encoded in the Book of Genesis. As God is the One who bestows providence, the words *and the Lord God made for Man* are crossing this word. The name of God, *Elohim*, is encoded exactly in the same location in skip -6. One line below is written *put forth his hand*. The congruent phrase *and the Lord had regard* is written in close proximity to the word *providence*.

```
נ י מ ו א ל א י ש כ ת ש ו ק ת כ ו ה ו א י מ ש ל ב כ ו ל א ד מ א מ ר כ י ש מ ע ת ל
כ ל מ מ נ ו א ר ו ר ה ה א ד מ ה ב ע ב ו ר כ ב ע צ ב ו נ ת א כ ל נ ה כ ל י מ י ח י
ע ת א פ י כ ת א כ ל ח מ ע ד ש ו ב כ א ל ה א ד מ ה כ י מ מ נ ה ל ק ח ת כ י ע פ ר
ו א ה י ת ה א מ כ ל ח י ר ה ע ש י ה ו ה א ל ה י מ ל א ד מ ו ל א ש ת ו כ ת נ ו ת ע
ד מ מ נ ו ל ד ע ת ט ו ב ו ר ע ו ע ת ה פ נ י ש ל ח י ד ר ו ל ק ח ג מ מ ע צ ה ח י י
ל ע ב ד א ת ה א ד מ ה א ש ר ל ק ח מ ש מ ו ג ר ש א ת ה א ד מ ו י ש כ נ מ ק ד מ ל
א ת ד ר כ ע צ ה ח י י מ ו ה א ד מ י ד ע א ת ח ו ה א ש ת ו ו ת ה ר ו ת ל ד א ת ק י
א ת ה ב ל ו י י ה י ה ב ל ר ע ה ר צ א נ ו ק י נ ה ע ב ד א ד מ ה ו י ה י מ ק צ י מ
א נ מ ה ו א מ ב כ ר ו ת צ א נ ו ו מ ח ל ב ה נ ו ר י ש ע י ה ו ה א ל ה ב ל ו א ל מ נ
י פ ל ו פ נ י ו ו י א מ ר י ה ו ה א ל ק י נ ל מ ה ח ר ה ל כ ו ל מ ה נ פ ל ו פ נ י
ב צ ו א ל י כ ת ש ו ק ת ו ו א ת ה ת מ ש ל ב ו ו י א מ ר ק י נ א ל ה ב ל א ח י ו ו
ה ו ר י א מ ר י ה ו ה א ל ק י נ א י ה ב ל א ח י כ ו י א מ ר ל א י ד ע ת י ה ש מ ר
```

○ *providence*
□ *Elohim*
▭ *and the Lord God made for Man*
__ *put forth his hand*
⌐ *and the Lord had regard*

As one goes up the spiritual ladder, one is confronted by numerous obstacles. These obstacles constitute challenging events in real life, for they prompt an individual to let go of the filth which is called egoism or self-love. Kabbalistically speaking, these challenges provide a person with the opportunity to limit what he receives for his own pleasure, in order to return light to the Creator (אור חוזר). God created Man so that he can receive light and experience pleasure. At the same time, God created in Man the possibility to give back light to the Creator. In other words, God gave Man the possibility to be exactly like Him. Evidently, the process of correcting of our souls (*tikun neshama*) is the purpose of creation.

An impressive matrix is generated by the minimal skip in the Torah, -4860, of the phrase *knew the Most High*, ידע עליון. Miraculously, this phrase accurately crosses the verse *and knows the knowledge of the Most High who sees the vision of the Almighty*. Coinciding with *knew the Most High* is written *the Lord's vengeance*, נקמת יהוה, and *the Lord execute judgment*. It is possible that God meant to address this array to people who have knowledge of the Lord's vengeance. Beside *knew the Most High* is encoded in the same skip the phrase *like my light*, הרי כאור שלי.

כבוריספחמשתועלירוראמלאינגאלונמכרבערכאכככלחרמאשרחרמאישל
מאדמעדבהמהליייהירואניייהוהורדבריהירהאלמשהבמדברסינילאמרפק
הורהאלמשהלאמרדברארלבנייישראלראמרתאלהמאישאישכיתשטהאשתורום
להשעירעזימאחדלחטאתולזבחהשלמימבקרשנימאילמחממשהעתדימחמש
הצרראתהכמוהרעתעתמבחצצרתונזכהתמלפנייהוהאלהיכמונושעתממאיב
נירומונהרמנימומונהתאנימלמקהרמההוראקראנחלאשכולעלאדותהאשכו
נירמאחריהמלמעלנתכרורועשיתמאתאלמצותיהירית מקדשימלאלהיכמא
דהומישאורענמחקתעולמלדרתיכמורבתוכבנריישראלאינחלרנחלהכי
דתעמכמושנתנבבניורפליטמנובנתירובשביתלמלראמריסיחורנונירמאבד
רונאמהגברשתמהעינאנאמשמעאמהיאלוידעועתעליורנמחזהשדיחזהנ
אשרנתתילבנייישראלוראיתהאתהרונאספתאלעמיכבגמאתהכאשרנאספאה
אנשימלצבאוריהירעלמדינלתתנקמתיהורהבמדינאלפלמטהאלפלמטהלכ
מאתאשרהכהיהוהבהמכלבכורובאלהיהמעשוהרוהשפטימרריסעובניייש
בנייישראלואדנייצורהביייהוהלתתאתנחלתצלפחדדאחנילובנתירוהירולא

○ knew the Most High
□ like my light
__ and knows the knowledge of the Most High who sees the vision of the Almighty
▭ the Lord's vengeance
⌐⌐ the Lord execute judgment

Kabbalah deals extensively with the subject of angels. The issue of angels is not simple because angels, although powerful, also have their limitations. Their strength emanates from their ability to perceive the quality of a potential setting. Their limitation, as far as we are concerned, has to do with their prohibition against opening a door for us. They are compelled to preserve our right of choice and therefore, they must let us act on our own. An appropriate metaphor for this situation is the man who can take a horse to water but is not able to make him drink. God's blueprint provides a person with favourable settings, as well as less favourable ones, which means that one scenario may be pertinent, another should be avoided, and some are neutral.

Kabbalah tells us that there are four universes. One of them is called the Universe of *Yetzirah* (Formation), and all angels come from this universe. The angel Metatron reigns over the Universe of *Yetzirah*, which is sometimes called "The Universe of Metatron." The minimal appearance in the Torah of the words *angel of purity*, מלאך טהרה, in skip 10888, coincides in close proximity with the name *Metatron*, מטטרון. Together with the name *Metatron* is written in text *behold, my angel shall go before you*. Rabbi Aryeh Kaplan writes in his book, *Meditation and Kabbalah*, concerning God's spokesman: "In many places in the Bible we find that an angel speaks in God's name, and this is the inner meaning of what God said regarding an angel, 'My Name is in him' (Exodus 23:21). This angel is usually identified as Metatron, and regarding this angel, the Talmud says, 'his name is like that of his Master.'"

```
רצמצרימויקראפרעהשמיוספצפנתפענחוריתנלואתאסנתבתפ
רימאיששדהוכיחזקעלהמהרעבותהיהארצלפרעהואתהעמהעב
ישקרויצאונגשיהעמושטריוויאמרואלהעמלאמרכהאמרפרע
זההוצאתיאתהצבאותיכממארצמצרימושמרתמאתהיומהזהלדר
מעובקליושמרתמאתהבריתיוהייתמליסגלהמכלהעמימכיליכ
חמרצפיתאתהברחמזהבוהקמתאתהמשכנכמשפטואשרהראיתב
כנזההאתהעמאלאשרדברתילכהמלאכיילכלפניכרביומפקד
ישעלשמדולשנימעשרשבטוריעשועלהחשנשרשרתגבלתמעשהעבת
חירורזאתהתורתזבחהשלמימאשריקריבליהוההאמעלתולדיהיקרי
אהצרעתעורבשראישצרועהואטמאהואטמאיטמאנוהכהנבראש
אשמלפניריהוהעלחטאתואשרחטאונסלחלומחטאתואשרחטאוכ
שנימלפיהניישינבגאלתומכסספקנתוואממעטנשארבשנימעדש
תראתהמנקיתואתקשותהנסכולהחמההתמידעליריהיהופרשועל
עדובארבעהעשריומבחדשהזהבינהערבימתעשואתובמעדוככ
```

○ *Metatron*
□ *angel of purity*
▭ *behold, my angel shall go before you*

According to the Jewish calendar, we are now in the year 5761, which means that we are approaching the end of the sixth millennium. Hence, the issue of the Messiah becomes relevant. In gematria, the words *Messiah* and *snake* have the same numeric value of 358. Although there has always been great animosity between humans and snakes, Kabbalah elucidates on the subject of Adam and Eve and the snake in Garden of Eden. Literally understood, the snake in the Garden of Eden assumes the role of a troublemaker. As Rabbi David Cooper writes, many of the Torah commentators were bothered by this issue, for, what does a troublemaker do in a paradise to begin with? God cursed the snake but "Everybody agreed, however, that the curse does not make sense the way it is written; indeed, the language of comparison mitigates the power of the curse…. According to this way of looking at things, we are currently in the heel phase of a six-thousand-year cycle…. The serpent biting at our heels indicates that we are moving closer to the realization of messianic consciousness…. From this Kabbalistic perspective, the serpent is the vehicle for messianic consciousness. Thus the serpent represents far more in mystical Judaism than is commonly known, and a deeper understanding of these teachings changes entirely our appreciation of the story of creation" (Cooper, 1997). In the Torah, a serpent made of copper functions as a savior. In the Book of Numbers 21:8, God commands Moses: *Make yourself a serpent, and set it upon a pole; and it shall come to pass, that whoever is bitten shall look at it, and he shall live.*

An interesting matrix is generated by the word *Messiah snake*, as one word written back to back, *Messiah ekans*, משיח שחנ, in its minimal skip in the Torah, 350. As if to symbolize that human beings and snakes are adversaries, the words *Messiah* and *snake* are encoded here facing each other. This word is encoded at the beginning of the Book of Genesis, and the word *snake* in plain text accurately crosses the encoded word *snake*. Furthermore, the word *snake* is encoded again, next and in parallel to the word *Messiah*. The phrase *every creeping thing that creeps upon the earth* is crossing the word *Messiah snake*. One line above the latter is written *the big reptiles*.

○ *messiah snake* ▭ *snake* ⬠ *snake*
⊔ *every creeping thing that creeps upon the earth* ⊓ *the big reptiles*

שלישיויאמראלהימיהימארתברקיעהשמימלהבדילביןנהיומו
יירקיעהשמימויברבראאלהימאתהתנינמהגדלימואתכלנפשהחיה
ובבהמהובכלהארצובכלהרמשהרמשעלהארצויברבראאלהימאתהא
דויהיערבויהיבקרימהששויכלוהשמימוהארצוכלצבאמוי
נהאדמהויפחבאפיונשמתחייימויהיהאדמלנפשחיהויטעיהוה
קהיהוהאלהימאתהאדמויניחהובבגנגנעדנלעבדהולשמרהויצוירה
יריקחאחתמצלעתיויסגרבשרתחתנהויבניהוהאלהימאתהצלע
תנעוברופנתמתוניואמרהנחשאלהאשהלאמותתמתונכיידעאלה
שמעתיבגנואיראכיעירמאנכיואחבאואיאמרמיהגידלככיעיר
יבנימואלאישכתשוקתכוהואימשלבכולדאמראמרכישמעתלקול

A powerful tool which is used when practising Kabbalah is permutation of letters. In the following matrix you can see the relevant phrases which coincide with permutation of two names of God. In the Book of Exodus, chapter 3, verses 13-14, Moses asks God what should he answer when people ask what is God's name: *And God said to Moses, I Am Who I Am* (*Eheye asher Eheye* אהיה אשר אהיה).

Permutation of the names *Elohim* (אלהים) and *Eheye* (אהיה) is אאלההייהם. We take the first letter of the name *Elohim*, then the first letter of the name *Eheye*, then the second letter of the name *Elohim*, then the second letter of the name *Eheye*, etc. In English it would look like this: *Eelhoehyiem*. The minimal appearance of this permutation in the Torah is encoded in skip 3575 towards the end of the Book of Deuteronomy. Crossing the permutation is written *the beauty of His name*, and in close proximity is written in text *God* and five times *The Lord your God*.

חריאלהימאחרימועבדתמוהשתחויתלהמהעדיתיבכמהיומכיאבדתאבדו ן
ברדפמאחריכמוביאבדמויהוהעדהיומהזהואשרעשהלכמבמדברעדבאכמעד
יהוהאלהיכאתהגויאמאשראתהבאשמהלרשתאותממפניכוירישתאתממוישבת
תשלחנוחפשימעמכוכיתשלחנוחפשמעמכלאתשלחנוריקמהענירקתעניק
כחלקיאכלולבדממכריועלהאבוותמאתהבאאלהארצאשרי הוהאלהיכנתן
שראלונכפרלהמהדמואתהתבערהרדמהנ קימקרבכביתעשהישרבעיניריהו
ועשיתכאשרנדרתלירהואלהיכונדהאשרדברתבפיככיתבאבברכרמעכבוא ב
נעלכלהגויאמאשרעשהלתהלהלהוטשמולתפארתלהיתכעמקדשליהוהאלהיכ
כלאותולמלמופתוברזרעכעדעולמתחתאשראבעדתאתאעלאעבדלאבבשמחהוב
כמאבתיכומלייהוהאלהיכאתלבבברזרעכלאהבהאתאל יהוהאלהיכבכב
עלאברתויהוהבהדדינחנוואינעמואלנכרירכבהועלבמותיארצויאכלת

○ *permutation of two names: Elohim and Eheye*   ▭ *the beauty of His name*

⊏⊐ *the Lord your God*   ⊔ *God*

Although this book is not about its author, I will have the reader know that while researching the Code, I discovered that my name is meticulously encoded in the Torah. In a way, the appearance of my encoded name has been a source of embarrassment to me. Nevertheless, I decided to publish a part of this material, for an extraordinary piece of information emerged by researching the Code by means of permutation of letters: I was able to discover the reincarnation of my soul.

The following four tables show that indeed, it is the author of this book who is encoded in these matrices, for no other Dan Harlap was born on the ninth of Sivan, 5707 (May 28, 1947). A matrix from the very beginning of Genesis is generated by my full name in skip 1564. Beside the name *Dan Harlap*, דן חרלפ, is encoded the year in which I was born *5707* (1947) in skip -4, the second-minimal appearance of this word in the Torah. The words *the name of his brother* is crossing my name, and my brother's name (my only full brother), *Uli*, is encoded in the same location of the matrix. Barry Roffman calculated the probability of this matrix to be one in 169,156 (see appendix.).

```
אאלהימליבשהארצולמקוההמימקראימוריראאלהימכיטובויאמראל
כלפניהאדמהוייצריהוהאלהימאתהאדמעפרמנהאדמהוריפחבאפיונשמ
והאלהימלאשהמהזאתעשית ותאמרהאשהההנחשהשיאיואכלוויאמריהוה
הותלדעדהאתיהאביה ואהי האביישבאהלומקנהומשמאחרוליובלהואהיהאב
עצבוניודינומנהאדמהאשרארההיהוהריהוריחילמכאהולידואתנחחמש
מימעלהארצויבאנחובניוואשתונשיבניואתואהתבהמהפנימיהמבו
יממעלהארצויסרנחאתממכסהתבהבוויראוהנהחרבויהניהאדמהובחדשהש
רניתורערותאביהמלאראוריקצנחמיינורויודעאתאשרעשהלרבנוהקטנ
לאשרבבנרובניהאדמויאמריהוההנענמאחדושפהאחתלכלמוזההחלמלעשו
יראיהוהאלאברמויאמרלזרעכאתנאתהארצהזאתויבנשממזבחליהוה
```

○ *Dan Harlap*
□ *5707 (1947)*
⌐⌐ *the name of his brother*
⬠ *Uli*

My full name in its minimal skip in the Book of Genesis, -1048, coincides with the name of the city in which I was born, *Rehovot*, as well as the year of my birth, *707 (1947)*.

להנערויקראמלאכאלהימאלההגרמנהשמימויאמר
להוריקמוילכאלהמקומאשראמרלווהאלהימביומה
רמואתאכשדואתחזווואתפלדשואתידלפואתבתואל
אשתואלמערתשדההמכפלהעלפניממראהואחברון
ינאמעטמיממכדכותאמרשתהאדנירותמהרותרדכד
שרהתהלכתילפנירוישלחמלאכואתכוהצליחדרככ
לחוואתרבקהאחתמואתמקתהואתעבדאברהמואתא
שמומשמעוודומהומשאחדרותימאיטורנפישוקדמ
שראמראליכירברבארצהזאתואהיהעמכואברכככי
ליהויקראשמהרחברתיאמרכיעתהההרחירביההל
אנימצוהואתכלכנאאלהצאנוקחלימשמשנידידיע
ועשואחירובאמצידורישעגמהואמטעמימויבאלא

○ *Dan Harlap*
▭ *Rehovot*
□ *707 (1947)*

My name is encoded in the Torah either by my full name or in the Book of Numbers, where my family name is encoded in its minimal skip, 4, and the word *the family* is written with it. In the matrix generated by my date of birth, nine Sivan, ט סיון, (day and month as one word) in skip 6199, is encoded my family name in the minimal skip sequence in the Torah, 4, and through it, in plain text, the word *the family*. Beside my date of birth is written my first name, *Dan*, and the year of my birth is also encoded in close proximity. Just beside my date of birth written in plain text is the word *code*. I faxed a few matrices to professor Eliyahu Rips. He confirmed that these matrices are significant and impressive.

תתיאתוואתכלעמדוואתארצוועשיתלוכאאשרעשיתלסיחנמל
ונילכרמימשמפחתהכרמיאלהמשחתםירהראובניוריהיופקדיה
כבשיומבמסספרמכמשפטועירעדזימאחדחטאתמלבדעלתהתמי
לחציושבטמנשהבניוסיפאתממלכתסיחנמלכהאמריואתממלכ
ימאשרדברמשהאלכליראלבעלברהירזבמדברבערבהמולס
שאעירניכימהוצפנהוחיימנהונמדרחההראההבעיניככילאתע
עהובכלביתולעיניוירואותניוהוציאמוצימדלמענהביאאתנו
ככוכרביהשמימלרבואהבתאתיהוהאלהיכושמרתמשמרתוו
עשרדגנכתירשכויצהרשויברכתבברכרכובצאנכלמענתלמדליר

○ *nine Sivan*	□ *Harlap*	___ *the family*
⬠ *Dan*	◇ *707 (1947)*	▭ *code*

A similar matrix exists in skip 763. In this matrix, just below the name *Harlap*, is written in plain text *Dan of the family*. That my name is encoded in relation to the coming holocaust can be seen in this matrix. The expression *the holocaust is really coming* (partly seen due to the length of the expression) contains the passage *Dan of the family*. Indeed, the Torah Code has provided me with a certain Kabbalistic perspective of where we are and where we are heading, as well as the ability to comprehend the premise on which the Lights operate: The extreme delicacy of God's blueprint of creation versus the absolute of God's intentions.

```
יתנ ו ממצר ימלמ ותבמדברכיאי נלחמ ואי נמימו נפשנ רקצהבלחמהקלקלו
לכהאמרי לאמראעברהבארצכלאנ ט הבשדהובכרמלאנ שתהמיבארבדרכהמל
שאיר לושרירדויירשואתארצ ו וס עו בני ישראלויחנ ובערבותמ ואבמעב
יהוהלתתילהלכעמכמויקומ וש ת מ ואביבאולאלבלקריאמרומ אנ בלעמה
וי חראפבלעמ ויכאתהאת ו נבמק ל פתחיהוהאתפיהאת ו נ ותאמ רלבלעממ
אוקרי תחצ ותויזהבלקברוצא א ישלחלבלעמ ולשרימ אשראת ו ויהיבב
ימ אלראשהפסגהויבנשבעהמזבח תיעלפר ואילבמ בחוריאמראלבלקהתי
ברכאתישראל ולאהלכככפענמ בפעמלקראתנ חשימ ורישתאלהמדברפנ יוויש א
השדייחזהנפלוגלוריעי נימ אר אנ ו ולאעתה אש רנ ו ולאקר ובדרכ וכבמ
תשנ המ אתאישישראל ואתהאשהאלקבתהותעצרהמ גפהמעלבני ישראלויה
החצרונ ילכרמי מש ח ת ה כ רמי אל המשפ חת ימ אלהמשפ חת נ ופד י המשלשהו
תהישבי לשמ רנ מ שפ חתהתהשמ רנ י אלהמשפ חתיששכרלפקד י המ ארבעה ושש ימ א
ח מ שהוארבע י מ א ל פ ושמ א ותא צא נ י ד נ למ שפ חת ל ש ו חממשפ חתהתהשו ח מ
ל ו י במצ ר ימ ותלד לעמ ר מ אתאהר נ ו אתמשה ו אתמר ימ אחתמ ו רולד לאהר נ את
```

○ nine Sivan
□ Harlap
__ the family
☐ Dan of the family
◇ 5707 (1947)
⬠ the holocaust is really coming

At the beginning of the morning prayer, in the part of blessings of the Torah, we thank God for our souls: "My God, the soul You placed within me is pure…." In this instance, while saying the word 'soul', a person is allowed to permute in his mind the letters of the word 'soul', *neshama*, נשמה, with the letters of his given name. Such permutation begins with the first letter of his name, then the first letter of the word 'soul', then comes the second letter of his name, then the second letter of the word 'soul', etc. In my case, the name Dan in Hebrew contains two letters, and the second letter of Dan is the same first letter of the word 'soul'. Consequently, the new word which is created by this permutation is *Dansoul*, דננשמה.

You should know that this is not a little game of letters and words. Rather, this permutation represents a powerful way of referring to the specific soul which lives in a person. Using the word דננשמה (*Dansoul*) with the Torah Code, I wondered whether or not I would be able to figure out my previous reincarnation. To the best of my understanding, as my name is exquisitely encoded in the Torah, this would be the most efficient and reliable form of practising Kabbalah as far as the area of reincarnation is concerned.

In the Hebrew calendar, I was born in the year תשז which is the number 707. Indeed, the word דננשמה (*Dansoul*) is encoded in the Book of Numbers in skip sequence 707. This discovery is very specific, especially in light of the fact that above the word דננשמה (*Dansoul*) is encoded my family name, Harlap, in its minimal skip in the Torah, 4, with the word *of family* written through it in plain text. Furthermore, this discovery is meaningful because next to the word דננשמה (*Dansoul*) coincides the congruent phrase *a man in whom is the spirit.*

In the eighteenth century lived a Jewish sage, a giant in the world of Judaism and Kabbalah. His name was Rabbi Moshe Chayim Luzzatto. He has been known in his abbreviatory name Ramchal, רמחל. According to *Margalioth Encyclopedia* (page 1095), Ramchal was born in 1707/5467 (exact date unknown). He died on the 26 of Iyar, 1747/5507. The Ramchal institution in Jerusalem confirmed this data.

In the following matrix, generated by the word דננשמה (*Dansoul*) in skip 707 which represents the year of my birth, is encoded my family name in its minimal skip 4. Crossing the word *Dansoul* is written *a man in whom is spirit*. The name *Ramchal* is also encoded in skip 707, sharing one letter with my family name. Ramchal and his family died in the year תקז (1747) in the city of Acre, עכו, in a plague. In close proximity to the name *Ramchal* is written in text *those that died in the plague* and is encoded the word *in Acre*. The year of his death is encoded crossing the name *Ramchal*. Just under the names *Ramchal* and *Harlap* is encoded, again in skip 707, the word *your soul*, as if clearly saying: *Your soul, Harlap, is the soul of Ramchal.*

The 26 of Iyar, *Ramchal's* death, was Saturday. In Hebrew, Saturday, Sabbath, is the seventh day of the week. In this matrix, the words *in the seventh day* are crossing the word דננשמה (*Dansoul*). I was born on May 28, 1947, which was a Wednesday. In Hebrew, Wednesday is called 'fourth day'. The words *in the fourth day* are also crossing the word דננשמה (*Dansoul*). In the line between *in the seventh day* and *in the fourth day* is written *year number seven*. The number 7 appears numerous times, in the Hebrew calendar as well as in the Gregorian, both for our years of birth and *Ramchal's* year of death. In the Hebrew calendar, the number 7 appears twice in my year of birth, 707, once in the *Ramchal's* year of birth, 467, and once in his year of death, 507. In the Gregorian calendar, the number 7 appears four times in *Ramchal's* years of birth and death, 1707, 1747, and once in my year of birth, 1947.

מאלבבלעמויאמראליואתשבעעתהמזבחתערכתיואעלפרואילבמזבחורשמיהוהדב
זבובבנאדמויתנחמההוואאמרולאיעשהודבולגלאיקימנהנהברכלקקחתיוברכול
ייותהנפלויגלויעינימהטבואהלכלעקבמשכנתיכישראלככנחלימנטיוכנגת
היהירשהשעיראיבויוישראלעשתחילויורדמיעקבוהאברדשרידמעירוריראאתע
ריהיוהמתימבמגנפהאתבאלהועשריואלפורידבריהוהאלמשהלאמרפינחסבנאלעז
נמשפחתהחצרונילכרמישמשפחתההקמיאלמשפחתהראובניוייהיופקדיהמשלשה
פוחמשמאותובניישששכרלמשפחחתמתולעמשפחתהתולעלפוהמשפתהפונילישוב
לאחירממשפחתהאחירמילשפופמפופמפשפחתהשופמילחופמשפחתחתההופמיוריהירבנ
טואלהפקודידיהלוילמשפחתמלגרשונמשפחתהגרשנילקהתמשפחתהקהתילמרדרים
תבמדברורוהואלאהיהבתוכהעדאתהחנועדימעליהוהבעדתקרחכיבחטאומתובנבנימל
אינלהמרעהויאמריהוהאלאלמשהקחלכאתיהושעבננאישאשרוחבנורסמכתאתי
ימבניישנהתמימימומושניעשרנימסלתמנחהבלולהבשמןנסכיועלתהשבתועלע
ריחניוחחליהוהעלעולתהתמידיעשהונסכולביומהבריעימקראקדשיהיהלכמכ
ניחחפרבנבנבקראהדאילאחדכבשימבניושוגגשנהתמיומיהיולכמומנחתמסלתבל
עירחטטאאתהאחדמלבדעלתהתמידונמנחתהתמיידומנחתהונסכהובביעירביעימעשרהאירלמשנ
להתעשולייהוהבמועדיכמלבדמנדריכמונדבתכמלעלתיכמולמנחתיכמולנסכ

○ *Dansoul*   ⌐ *a man in whom is spirit*   △ *Harlap*

— *the family*   ○ *Ramchal*   ⬡ *your soul*

▭ *those that died in the plague*   ▽ *in Acre*   ◇ *507 (1747)*

⌐ *Saturday*   - - - *Wednesday*   ⬠ *year number seven*

Another peculiar connection is the following: The 26 of Iyar in the year 507, Ramchal's death, corresponds to May 6, 1747. Although Ramchal died, not was born on the 26 of Iyar, it so happens that the date 26 of Iyar in the year of Ramchal's birth, 1707, is May 28, and May 28 is the date of my birth in the Gregorian calendar.

In the epilogue to his famous book, *Mesilat Yesharim* (*Path of the Just*), Ramchal thanks God for helping him publish his book. Ramchal published the book *Mesilat Yesharim* in Amsterdam in the year 1740. He did not mean to stay in Amsterdam, for his goal was to reside in the Holy Land. Three years thereafter Ramchal and his family moved to the city Acre, in Israel. Astonishingly, in the epilogue Ramchal adds that his consolation would be in a place he called Rehovot. Two hundred seven years thereafter I was born in Rehovot. The town Rehovot did not exist in 1740.

Is it possible to know which soul reincarnated in Ramchal? Yes, in this case it is. In Hebrew, the word alive is חי. The gematria of the word חי is 18. In the following matrix, the connection between Ramchal and his reincarnation has to do with the number eighteen: eighteen lines above the phrase *those that died in the plague* appears again this exact phrase, *those that died in the plague*. This identical phrase serves here as an indication to connect one life to a previous life. And there, in this area of the matrix, we find another great Kabbalist, another giant in the world of Judaism – Rabbi Moshe Cordovero, or in his abbreviatory name, Ramak. Under the phrase *those that died in the plague* is encoded the name *Ramak*, also in skip –18. In the same line is written *will die*. And eighteen lines below the name *Ramak* is encoded the first letter of the name *Ramchal*, as well as the name *Harlap*. Interestingly, Ramak lived 180 years before Ramchal; again, the number eighteen. Although Ramak wrote a great deal about Kabbalah, very little is known about his life. We only know that Ramak was born in the year 5282, הרפב, (1522) and died in the city of *Tzfat*, צפת, in Israel, in the year 5330, השל, (1570).

The only place in the Torah where the year 5282, הרפב, is encoded back and fourth, as one word in its minimal skip 3, is in the same line which reads *those that died in the plague*. This means that the year 5282, הרפב, (1522) becomes a word of seven letters בפרהרפב, and you can read the year 5282, הרפב, in equal interval 3, from the centre, backwards and forwards. It is as if the year of *Ramak's* birth were written twice in numbers, using the Gregorian calendar, as 225<u>1</u>522. One line above the phrase *those that died in the plague* and the year of *Ramak's* birth is encoded in the same skip sequence of the words דננשמה (*Dansoul*), and *Ramchal*, 707, the word *his soul*. In close proximity is encoded the name *Ramak* in skip 707, the name of the city *Tzfat*, and just above it, the word *town*. The year of *Ramak's* death, השל, is encoded in compact configuration with the name of the city *Tzfat*. Interestingly, *Ramak* was one of the only Kabbalists who specifically referred to the Torah Code in skipping of letters. As quoted in the first chapter, in his book, *Pardes Rimonim* (*Orchard of Pomegranates*), which is one of the most important of all Kabbalah classics, *Ramak* writes that "The secrets of our holy Torah are revealed through knowledge of combinations, numerology (gematria), switching letters, first-and-last letters, shapes of letters, first- and-last verses, *skipping of letters* (*dilug otiot*) and letter combinations. These matters are powerful, hidden and enormous secrets. Because of their great secrecy, we do not have the ability to fully comprehend them" (italics are mine).

מהוזרעויורשנהוהעמלקיוהכנעניושבבעמקמחרפנוסעולכמהם
ויהושעבנגונוכלבבניפנחיומנהאנשימההמההלכימלתוראתהאר
ניחללריהוהוכיתעשהבנבברעלהאוזבחללפלאנדראושלמימליהוה
דלעלהלריחניחחליהוחליהוהומנחתומנחתוונסכוכמשופטושעירום עזרימאחדלחטת
מציצתעלכנפיבגדידהמלדרחתמונתכועלציצתהכנפפתילתכלתוהיהל
ליולעבדאתהעבדתמשכניהוהולעמדלפניהעדהלשרתמויקרבאתכראת
עלכללהעדהתקצפויודבריהוהואלהאלשמלאמרדבראלהעדהלאמרהעלוטמסב
אלמשהלאמראמראלאלעזרבנאהרנהכהנוירמאתהמחתמביונהשרפהו
ריהיוהמתימבמגפהארבעתעשראלפושבעמאותמלבדהמתימעלדברקר
וכלנואבדנוכללהקרבהקרבאלמשכניהוהימאיתהאמתמנולגועויאמרי
דשיהיהלכוזהלהכתרומתמתנמלכלתנופתבנייישראללכנחתימולבני

○ *his soul*   ▽ ⬠ *Ramak*   □ *5282 (1522)*

○ *5330 (1570)*   ⊔ *town*   ⬠ *Tzfat*

▭ *those who died in the plague*   ⌐ *will die*

Interestingly, in 1990, professor Bracha Sack lectured in the World Congress of Jewish Studies about "The Influence of Rabbi Moshe Cordovero's [Ramak] writings on the Philosophy of Rabbi Moshe Luzzatto [Ramchal]." Both Kabbalists equally related to the topic of 'two realities'; the perfect world vis-à-vis the imperfect world. Both of them justified the creation of our imperfect world, one of good and evil which requires justice, so that later, the process of correction transforms our world to a perfect one. In other words, both analyzed the existence of the obvious world, the one of conflict, versus the existence of the invisible world, the one of reward. Ramak and Ramchal equally related to the material domain as something false, void and temporary. The real world is the invisible one, a world which hides behind our dark reality and can only be seen by a Kabbalist who understands the mystical methods and God's secrets.

Chapter 5
Glenn Gould, Rhythm and Ecstasy

Every human being, I guess, has his own way of escaping the jungle in which he lives. Mine is classical music. Somewhere along the pebble stones of a miserable childhood, I discovered the music of Bach. It constituted such a profoundly moving experience that I came to realize I had the ability to sense and experience with a remarkably high degree of intensity. Moreover, I was able to separate in my mind different instruments or different lines in a very clear way, focusing on a single part or on the whole, switching back and forth, mixing and separating, something that became a mental game, and a very gratifying one. I discovered listening was an active process, not a passive one. I let the music sink in deep, allowing it almost to take me over. It felt like the instrument engulfed my soul in such a way that nothing existed between myself and the music. And while with music my feelings were agitated, the outside world forgotten, I got to know myself. I was grateful for the richness of my interior life, for the inspiration, for being able to go inside myself at will to see and feel and survive. Maybe this is the reason I like the music of Glenn Gould best of all. As Geoffrey Payzant writes in his book, *Glenn Gould: Music and Mind* (1992), "Gould seems to experience everything at a very high level of awareness." Gould called it ecstasy, which for him meant "a solitary condition, an individual person's standing outside himself" (Payzant, 1992). I tend to think that Glenn Gould was right; mental solitude, whether or not one is physically alone, is unquestionably a condition for this kind of experience to take place.

There has never been another pianist like Glenn Gould and most probably, there never will be. Apart from his intellect, his marvelous technique and his sheer virtuosity, Gould was unique for his ability to hear sounds in his mind in a way other mortals could not: he heard contrapuntally. By hearing each polyphonic line separately, by considering each line independently, he prescribed them different weights, changed their tempi, their "rhythmic gasps and breaths," as he said (Payzant, 1992). Words cannot describe the transformation from an intrinsic tonality Gould experienced as a performer to the actual sonority we encounter as listeners. It is like trying to explain to a deaf person the sound of a clarinet. As each of us has one dominant side of our brain, pianists use one hand to play the melodic line, while the other one complements the hand that plays that melody. Glenn Gould played with both hands independently, with amazing fluency and freedom, gracefully interweaving contrapuntal lines. His music is not merely an interpretation of music scores. Rather, for Gould, the music score was raw material from which he created his own music. He started where everybody else had finished.

In the following matrix you can see the names *Glenn* and *Gould* encoded in one line, coinciding with the word *musician*.

שכנונסעונביגרשוניובנימררינשאיהמשכנונסעדגלמחנהראובנלצב
בלבאהממתויעלונבגבוריבאעדזהברונושמאחימנששיותלמיליזחרהעזנק
בשגגהוראמנופשאהתתחטאבשבגהוהקריבהעזבתשנתהלחטאתוכפרהכהנע
ראתהמשמרתאהלמועדלכלעבדתהאהליוזרלאיקרבראליכמושמרתהמאתמשמ
תמאתפילמימריבהקהאתהאהרנואתאהלעדזרבנוורהעלאתמהרההרוהפשטאת
חצותויזבהלבקבקרוצאנויושלחלבלבלעמולשרימאשראתוויהיבהידרויק
משמאותבניייהודהעראונדורימתעראונדוינבארצכנענויהירובנייהוד
כבשיוושעירחטאתאחדלכפרעליכממלבדעלתהבקראשרלעלתהתמידיתעש
ינדהיתחטאוכלאשרלאיבאבאשתעבירובמירוכבסתמהבגדיכמביומהשב
וברמנצרזיסעומרמנפרצויחנובלבבנהויסעומלבנהויחנוברתהויס
נחלהבניגדליגביאישראלאדניצורהביהוהתתאתנחלתצלפחדאחינולב
ובהלפנימהעמניקראולהמזמזימעמגדולורברומכעננקימירשמי
כלהההואאלקנאכיתוליידבנימוברניבנימורנושנתמבארצורהשחתמועשית
רלאאמרמההעדתוהחקירימוהמשפטימאשרצוהיהוהאלהינאתכמוראמרתלב
ימירומוארבעימליהלהחמללאאכלתיומימלאשתיתיעלכלחטאתכמאשרחט

○ *musician*   △ *Glenn*   □ *Gould*

Most pleasures accessible to human beings are associated with rhythms. Somewhere in our brain, regardless of the nature of the stimulus, no matter which of our senses is being used, there is a mysterious mechanism that perceives rhythmical activity as gratifying. Music is an obvious example and sexual intercourse is another. The rhythmic movement of the jaw as we eat is also associated with the satisfaction food brings. We breathe in rhythm, walk in rhythm and calm a baby with rhythmic movements. Likewise, I have never seen people in love who caress and touch each other in non-rhythmical strokes. And then there are less apparent rhythms, somewhat more sophisticated but not less potent, such as the ones in paintings. Cezanne knew this best of all; Picasso understood his compositions and Cubism followed. Ezra Pound knew this secret too and, in Paris, he taught rhythmical prose to Ernest Hemingway. What a coincidence! Both Cubism and some of the richest harmonic prose that consort with rhythm, were conceived in Paris, the city most identified with romance and love. The bullfight at its best is permeated with rhythm. Only when a bullfighter is able to dominate a bull by a succession of rhythmical passes will the public get exhilarated.

In 1960, when Glenn Gould recorded ten Brahms intermezzi, he told an interviewer that his recording was "the sexiest interpretation of Brahms intermezzi you have ever heard" (Friedrich, 1990). Gould, the master of rhythm, tempi and accentuation, surely knew what he was talking about. And he considered himself one of the most romantic people around.

I used to live in Toronto. Although I did not know Glenn Gould personally, he was an integral part of my life. I remember my shock upon watching the evening news when his death was announced. It was one of those moments when one recognizes the world has changed and must ask, "I wonder how life is going to be from now on?" I still have a video of this broadcast and am still left breathless when I watch it. Gould changed my life, as I am sure he changed the lives of many others. A few months after he died, I left Toronto. It looked like a coincidence back then, in 1982, but when I think of it now, maybe it wasn't. Unable to reconcile myself to his loss, I have become addicted to Gould's music. In his playing, there is magic in the evenness of the notes as well as in the separation between each one of them. Hence, Gould's music has always seemed to come straight from heaven. As there is hardly a day in which the enchanting sound of his Steinway CD318 is not heard in my room, for me, Glenn Gould is immortal. And I always hope that after we die, our souls can go places and hear music. Because if this is not the case, dying is really a bad business.

Bibliography

Ashlag, Y. *The Wisdom of the Kabbalah: Giving the Torah*. Jerusalem: The Research Center of the Kabbalah, 1982. (In Hebrew).

Belk, R.W. "The Sacred Meaning of Money." *Journal of Economic Psychology*. 11 (1990): 35-67.

Ben-Mimon, M. (Rambam). *A Guide to the Confused*. Jerusalem: Mossad Harav kook, 1977.

Berlin, I. *The Crooked Timber of Humanity*. London: Fontana Press, 1990.

Chomsky, N. *What Uncle Sam Really Wants*. Berkely, 1992.

- - - . *World Orders, Old and New*. London: Pluto Press, 1994.

Cooper, D. *God is a Verb: Kabbalah and the Practice of Mystical Judaism*. New York: Riverhead Books, 1997.

Dimen, M. "Money Love and Hate." *Psychoanalytic Dialogues*. 4 (1994): 69-100.

Drosnin, M. *The Bible Code*. New York: Simon & Schuster, 1997.

Eatwell, J. "The Global Money Trap: Can Clinton Master the Markets?" *American Prospect*. Winter (1993):118-126.

Freud, S. "An Autobiographical Study." *Historical and Expository Works on Psychoanalysis*. Vol. 15. London: The Penguin Freud Library, 1993.

- - -. "A Seventeen-Century Demonological Neurosis." *Art and Literature*. Vol. 14. London: The Penguin Freud Library, 1990.

- - -. "Character and Anal Erotism." *On Sexuality*. Vol. 7. London: Penguin Freud Library, 1991.

- - -. "Civilization and Its Discontents." *Civilization, Society and Religion*. Vol. 12. London: The Penguin Freud Library, 1991.

- - -. "On Beginning the Treatment." *The Freud Reader*. Edited by Peter Gay. London: Vintage Press, 1995.

- - -. "On Transformations of Instinct as Exemplified in Anal Erotism." *On Sexuality*. Vol. 7. London: The Penguin Freud Library, 1991.

- - -. *The Psychopatology of Every Day Life*. Vol. 5. London: The Penguin Freud Library, 1991.

Friedrich, O. *Glenn Gould: A Life and Variations*. London: Methuen, 1994.

Fromm, E. *To Have or To Be.* London: Abacus Press, 1995.

Gay, P. *A Godless Jew: Freud, Atheism, and the Making of Psychoanalysis.* Binghampton, New York: Vail-Ballou Press, 1987.

- - -. *Freud: A Life for Our Time.* London: Papermac, 1995.

Gilboa, M. *Y. Leibowitz: Ideas and Contradictions.* Negev, Israel: Ben-Gurion University, 1994. (In Hebrew).

Halamish, Y.S. *Treasure of The Sign of the Zodiac.* Bnei Brack, 1997. (In Hebrew).

Hallowell, E.M., and W.J. Grace. "Money Styles." *Money and Mind.* Edited by S. Klebanow and E.L. Lowenkopf. New York: Plentum Press, 1991. 15-26.

Haralick, R. and Gerlzon M. *Actuality in Skipping Letters in the Torah.* Jerusalem: Yerid Hasfarim, 1977. (In Hebrew)

Hegel, G.W.S. *Philosophy of Right.* New York: Oxford University Press, 1967.

Howard, P.K. *The Death of Common Sense.* New York: Randon House, 1994.

Jones, E. *The Life and Works of Sigmund Freud.* London: Penguin Books, 1993.

Kamenetzky, Rabbi M. "Raising Sinai." *Parasha Parables.* New York: Bentsh Press, Volume 3, issue 37, 1997.

Kaplan, A. *Meditation and Kabbalah.* Maine, Samuel Weiser, Inc., 1982.

Katz, M. *On Hidden Codes in the Torah.* Jerusalem: 1996.

Klebanow, S. "Power, Gender and Money." *Money and Mind.* Edited by S.Klebanow and E.L.Lowenkopf: New York, Plentum Press, 1991. 51-59.

Lamont, M. *Money, Morals and Manners. The Culture of the French and the Americans Upper-Middle Class.* Chicago: The University of Chicago Press, 1992.

Lind, C. *Something's Wrong Somewhere.* Halifax: Fernwood Publishing, 1995.

Luzzatto, M.H. *Path of the Just.* Jerusalem, Orot Hayim, 1988. (In Hebrew. First published in Amsterdam in 1740).

- - -. *The Way of God.* With interpretation of Katz, A.Y. Jerusalem: Feldheim Publishing, 1996. (In Hebrew).

Masson, Jeffrey Moussaieff, ed. *The Complete letters of Sigmund Freud to Wilhelm Fliess 1887-1904.* Cambridge: The Belknap Press, Harvard University, 1985.

Marx, Karl. *Capital I.* London: Penguin Books, 1990.

- - -. *Capital III.* London: Penguin Books, 1991.

- - -.   *Economic and Philosophic Manuscripts of 1844.* Buffalo:1987.

Michelson, D. "Reading the Torah with Equal Intervals." *B'Or Torah.* 6, 1987.

Paskauskas, R.,ed. *The Complete Correspondence of Sigmund Freud and Ernest Jones 1908-1939.* Cambridge: The Belknap Press, Harvard University, 1995.

Payzant, G. *Glenn Gould: Music and Mind.* Toronto: Key Porter Books, 1992.

Raphael, S.P. *Jewish Views of the Afterlife.* N.J.: Jason Aronson, Inc., 1996.

Rendon, M. "Money and the Left in Psychoanalysis." *Money and Mind.* Edited by S. Klebanow and E.L. Lowenkopf : New York. Plentum Press, 1991. 135-147.

Rips, E., D. Witztum and Y. Rosenberg. "Equidistant Letter Sequences in the Book of Genesis." *Statistical Science.* Vol.9 (3). August, 1994. 429-438.

Sack, B. *The Kabbalah of Rabbi Moshe Cordovero.* Jerusalem, University of Ben-Gurion in the Negev, 1995. (In Hebrew).

Satinover, J. *Cracking The Bible Code.* New York: William Marrow and Company, Inc. 1997.

Simmel, G. *The Philosophy of Money.* Edited by T. Bottomore and D. Frisby. London: Routledge and Kegan Paul Ltd., 1991.

Soros, G. *Soros on Soros: Staying Ahead of the Curve.* New York: John Wiley & Sons, Inc. 1995.

Spence, G. *From Freedom to Slavery: The Rebirth of Tyranny in America.* New York: St.Martin's Paperbacks, 1993.

Tuchman, B. *A Distant Mirror: The Calamitous 14th Century.* Suffolk, UK: Penguin Books, 1978.

Warner, S.L. "Sigmund Freud and Money." *Money and Mind.* Edited by S.Klebanow and E.L.Lowenkopf: New York, Plentum Press, 1991, 121-133.

Witztum, D. *The Additional Dimension.* Jerusalem: Ketamar Yifrah,1988. (In Hebrew).

Yaniv, S. *Secrets in the Torah.* Jerusalem, 1989. (In Hebrew).

Appendix

A few words about the mathematics of the Bible Code: At the time of writing this book there is no consensus among the members of the International Torah Code Society as to the measurement of compactness of words or phrases; nor is there a measurement to evaluate repetitions of encoding. Although a few formulas, scales and equations have been used to evaluate matrices, the truth is that, beyond basic commonsense, researching the Code is more an art than a science. While the scientific research on the Code during the last fifteen years has been extremely important, I feel that an understanding of the Code's perspectives and dynamics is even more important than mathematical calculations. A matrix resulting in a probability of one in a hundred may be as important as a matrix with a probability of one in a million. It is clear that God intended to encode information in a way that, as much as technically possible, such information would appear in close proximity. At the same time, it is also clear to me that He never had in mind to set mathematical rules to evaluate matrices. If there had been such mathematical rules, He would have encoded them in the Torah.

Another puzzling issue emanates from researching Torah-controlled texts. Some people think that if one finds a matrix in Tolstoy's *War and Peace* similar to a matrix found in the Torah, the former invalidates the latter. As if the Torah Code should be assessed by isolated matrices! Mainly, God encoded settings. A setting consists of a few matrices describing a specific subject. Can anyone produce a decisive set of matrices from *War and Peace*, or from any other Torah-controlled text, describing God's intention to avenge the covenant? Or, can one produce from a controlled text the whole setting of *Eliyahu's death*? Or the entire setting which is called *Dan Harlap* with his date and place of birth and his family members? Obviously not, because Tolstoy was Tolstoy and God is God. And as for the ridiculous claim that one can find whatever one wishes to find in the Code: Can anyone produce from the Torah a significant set of matrices showing that God intended not to avenge the covenant?

I asked Barry Roffman to calculate the probability of three matrices. The following one, from page 81, is generated by the expression *Eliyahu's murder* in its minimal skip in the Torah, -3362. The probability of all that is marked in this matrix is one in 232 billion.

A	B	C	D	E	F	G	H
ELIYAHU'S MURDER	SKIPS	NUMBER	DIVIDE BY	THE QUOTIENT	E QUOTIENT	POISSON EQUATION	EACH WORD
IS CONDITIONAL AXIS TERM	USED	IN	304805	EQUALS	X 96 LETTERS	PROBABILITY FOR	OR PHRASE
SKIP N = 3,362	ON	CONTROL	LETTERS	FREQUENCY	EQUALS	THE WORD	HAS 1 CHANCE
	ELI		IN THE	PER LETTER	WORD	APPEARING	IN THE
	PLOT		CONTROL		EXPECTANCY	AT LEAST ONCE	FOLLOWING OF
							BEING HERE
MURDER @ SKIPS 1,-1, N, -N	-1	104	304805	0.000341202	0.032755368	0.032224721	31.03207852
OF THE FAMILY @ SKIP +1	1	75	304805	0.000246059	0.02362166	0.023344852	42.83599623
YAFFE @ SKIPS =1, -1, N, -N	3362	93	304805	0.000305113	0.029290858	0.028866039	34.64278585
THE MAN WITH 1 EYE @ +`1	1	2	304805	6.56157E-06	0.000629911	0.000629713	1588.026094
YOUR SINS MADE KNOWN @ +1	1	1	304805	3.28079E-06	0.000314955	0.000314906	3175.55211
						COMBINED	
						PROBABILITY =	
						4.30616E-12	
						THE ABOVE IS ONE	
						CHANCE IN	
						2.32225E+11	

The following calculation pertains to the matrix from page 82, generated by the expression *Yaffe's murder* in its minimal skip in the Torah, 369. The probability of the four markings appearing in such close proximity is one in 1,522,071,021.

A	B	C	D	E	F	G	H
YAFFE'S MURDER	SKIPS	NUMBER	DIVIDE BY	THE QUOTIENT	E QUOTIENT	POISSON EQUATION	EACH WORD
IS CONDITIONAL AXIS TERM	USED	IN	304805	EQUALS	X 63 LETTERS	PROBABILITY FOR	OR PHRASE
SKIP N = 369	ON	CONTROL	LETTERS	FREQUENCY	EQUALS	THE WORD	HAS 1 CHANCE
	ELI		IN THE	PER LETTER	WORD	APPEARING	IN THE
	PLOT		CONTROL		EXPECTANCY	AT LEAST ONCE	FOLLOWING OF
							BEING HERE
JERUSALEM @ SKIPS +1, -1, N, -N	369	1	304805	3.28079E-06	0.00020669	0.000206668	4838.67462
OF THE FAMILY @ SKIP +1	1	75	304805	0.000246059	0.015501714	0.015382181	65.01028651
THE DEATH OF WITNESS @ +1	1	1	304805	3.28079E-06	0.00020669	0.000206668	4838.67462
						COMBINED	
						PROBABILITY =	
						6.57E-10	
						THE ABOVE IS ONE	
						CHANCE IN	
						1522071021	

This calculation was performed on the encoding of my full name in skip 1564 (page 102), coinciding with the written phrase *the name of his brother*, and the encoded name *Uli*. Barry Roffman found the probability of this happening to be one in 169,156.

A	B	C	D	E	F	G	H
DAN HARLAP	SKIPS	NUMBER	DIVIDE BY	THE QUOTIENT	E QUOTIENT	POISSON EQUATION	CHANCE FOR EACH
S CONDITIONAL	USED	IN	304804	EQUALS	TIMES 42	PROBABILITY FOR	INDIVIDUAL TERM
AXIS TERM	ON	CONTROL	LETTERS	FREQUENCY	EQUALS	THE WORD	TO BE ON THE PLOT
	HARLAP		IN THE	PER LETTER	WORD	APPEARING	EQUALS ONE IN
	PLOT		CONTROL		EXPECTANCY	AT LEAST ONCE	
ULI @ -1563 to -1576	-1563	26	304805	8.53004E-05	0.003582618	0.003576208	279.6257564
NAME OF BROTHER @1	1	4	304805	1.31231E-05	0.000551172	0.00055102	1814.815522
						THE COMBINED	
						PROBABILITY =	
						1.97056E-06	
						THE ABOVE =	
						ONE CHANCE IN	
						507469.1631	
						DIVIDE ABOVE BY	
						3 DUE TO	
						TWO LOWER	
						SKIP FINDS FOR	
						DAN HARLAP.	
						REVISED FIGURE	
						EQUALS IN CHANCE IN	
						169156.3877	